Sexuality
and the
Counseling
Pastor

Sexuality and the Counseling Pastor

Herbert W. Stroup, Jr. &
Norma Schweitzer Wood

FORTRESS PRESS   Philadelphia

Library of Congress Catalog Card Number 73-88344

ISBN 0-8006-0264-1

4065I73   Printed in U.S.A.   1-264

To: **Barbara**

       Denise

       Heather

       Jenny

       Kate

       Kirk

       Scott

       Woody

Contents

Preface

During an interview with Dr. Tilla Vahanian in New York concerning supervision in marriage counseling, she asked us two important questions: "What are the limitations imposed by your religious tradition?" and "In view of the limitations, how do you plan to deal with the realities of contemporary marriage?"

As we formulated answers, we remembered how often we had confronted these same questions in contexts related to human sexuality. The questions come to us from counselees and students in our seminary classes, from pastors in our marriage counseling workshops and couples we meet as cotherapists in marriage counseling. All the questions in some way deal with the difficulties encountered in translating the Christian tradition concerning sexuality to the realities of the contemporary situation.

This book is our answer to these questions. We have addressed ourselves in the first instance to the parish pastor who, in one of his several roles, serves as a counselor. The term "counseling pastor" is intended to distinguish the pastor who counsels from the increasingly specialized minister, the "pastoral counselor," who usually works in a counseling center rather than in a parish. Even where we use the terms interchangeably, our primary reference is always to the pastor counseling in a parish. Furthermore, while the book is addressed primarily to the parish pastor, we think it has value also for seminary classes and for the counseling profession in general, which increasingly talks in terms of values in human sexuality.

Our method of address is by case studies based on actual situations involving real people. The cases presented are excerpted from clinical experience, case notes, and tapes. They represent a composite of persons and situations, with the privacy of the counselee preserved at all points.

We take an approach to the cases that is balanced, hopefully, between the clinical and the theoretical. It is necessary to deal with the biblical-theological tradition in human sexuality if the counseling pastor is to be the translator of this tradition to contemporary man. At the same time, we have given equal consideration to counseling styles and techniques. This dual approach represents an effort to respond to the seminary students and pastors who, having analyzed the presenting case and the thrust of the tradition, always ask, "Yes, but what do you *do* about it?"

Despite our deep concern for women as full partners and participants in the life of the church and the world, we have left out much that needs to be said about and for them. Two difficulties plagued us as we wrote. First, we felt the limitations of the English language. Short of using the cumbersome split-pronoun he/she, him/her, there was no clear way of indicating that the book is addressed to women pastors as well as to men. Second, limitations on book size dictated greater attention to general problem areas than to special interests. At present, the inroads by women into the pastoral ministry are small but vital. As more women assume what has been traditionally a male role, special problems will appear which we have not anticipated. How congregations and fellow pastors will respond to this new phenomenon in affirmation of person over gender only the future can disclose.

We are indebted to Dr. Donald R. Heiges, president of Lutheran Theological Seminary, Gettysburg, Pennsylvania. His Christian sensitivity to persons and to the role of women in theological education created the atmosphere which made possible this project and our joint work at the seminary.

A special word of gratitude is due to Dr. William B. Oglesby, Jr. of Union Theological Seminary in Richmond, Virginia, who read sections of the manuscript and made cogent suggestions for both direction and style; to M. Lucille Brennan for providing insight into the social problems of singles; to Dr. Eric W. Gritsch, who was our wise and sympathetic guide at moments of crisis; to Barbara K. Stroup for helping us make the English language say what we wanted it to say; and to Jeanne L. Nunamaker, registrar at Gettysburg Seminary, for her proficient and skilled work on the manuscript. None of the above persons is responsible, however, for positions taken in the book; that responsibility lies with the writers.

Herbert W. Stroup, Jr.

Norma Schweitzer Wood

Gettysburg, Pennsylvania
June, 1973

1. The Pastoral Encounter with Human Sexuality

Patrick and Priscilla Jones sit in the pastor's office, where they have been each Wednesday evening for five weeks. To stay married and to love is hard work and the Joneses are engaged in that work.

"No matter how hard I try to understand, I just can't respond to him. Somehow it just seems wrong and I can't do it."

But the pastor barely hears her words, for he heard them from his own wife (heaven forbid that the congregation should know that!) just the night before. And he looks at the Joneses and wonders why they came to him. It is their problem; but it is also his—and his wife's. And what is he to say?

Carol Brown puts it simply and quietly: "The children are young but not so young that a baby-sitter can't be with them during the day. And I do so much want to get back into social work where I can be alive and grow again; not to mention how that extra salary will help our budget.

"But Alan doesn't see it that way. He was raised differently and he has a different picture of me as a wife and mother. He loves me and he wants to help me, but . . . well . . . not this far.

"Pastor, tell me: Am I wrong? Is it my Christian duty to stay home with the children? Am I being unfair to Alan? What does God expect of me and my life? Or isn't that the issue?"

And the pastor thinks to himself, "What, indeed, does God expect for your life? What, indeed? And what shall I say?"

They seem so young and yet so wise and mature, this couple sitting in the pastor's study with the disturbing request. Graduate students at the local university, they plan to get married in about a year. But until then there is just no way: obligations and duties prevent marriage, and a scholarship requires the recipient to remain single. Yet there is an apartment in which they could live together for a year; and it would be cheaper for them, and their friends are doing it, and . . . is it wrong if they love each other and plan to marry?

So they make their request: "Would you be willing to construct with us a sort of public betrothal ceremony—a blessing on a one-year arrangement in which our intention to marry is clearly stated?"

And the pastor thinks to himself as he prepares his answer: "What is marriage? A promise from each to the other or two signatures on a legal document? Or both? And how do I decide?"

"There was just no point in going to my doctor about this; I think the problem needs something more than my doctor can give me."

Mrs. Dora Smith was obviously uncomfortable as she said, "I'm sure my fourteen-year-old son is masturbating. The whole thought disturbs me but I've seen the evidence. Pastor, what can I do to get him to stop?"

In the very way she asks the question she expresses a judgment and the pastor knows the answer she expects from him. But how can he give her a supporting answer when he knows the normality of the practice, particularly in an adolescent boy? What determines the priority of his answer? What will she tell her friends about what he says? What is he to say?

Each of these situations is concerned with human sexuality, and each makes its peculiar demand on the counseling pastor. But in all four cases the pastoral counselor is called upon to exercise a skill unique to his role. He is to translate the Christian heritage and tradition in human sexuality into meaningful thought forms and behaviors for contemporary people.

This requirement is unique to the pastoral counselor as compared with the psychological or psychiatric counselor. In the case of the latter, the material to be translated is the specialized knowledge on the subject found in the behavioral and medical sciences. Through the medium of the therapist, this knowledge is brought to bear directly upon the case at hand. The major concern in this translation is the therapeutic value of that knowledge for the patient. And while the therapist may stand within a particular tradition—Freudian, Rogerian, and the like—which binds him in style or content, that tradition also provides him with direct linkage to the problem at hand. Furthermore, he uses his particular tradition to facilitate his work.

The pastoral counselor, as any other counselor, needs to know and transmit pertinent knowledge from the behavioral sciences. But when he turns to the translation of the tradition in which he stands, he faces several distinctive problems.

First, the linkage between the tradition and the problem at hand is often obscure. As in all hermeneutical exercises, the correlation between the thought forms of the ancient world and those of the contemporary world is difficult to establish and sometimes only thinly apparent. It is much easier for the psychological counselor to move Freud's Vienna to the United States than it is for the pastoral counselor to bring Paul's Corinth to America. This is not to imply that the crucial dimension in translation is the factor of time-distance; rather, it is to suggest that both the nature and the intention of the traditions are different.

Second, the Christian tradition and heritage in human sexuality is of a mixed nature, and this complicates the process of translation. While there is strong affirmation of human sexuality in the biblical-theological tradition, the negative aspects, partly through acculturation, have been more prominent throughout the centuries of development. Thus, the pastoral counselor finds the more common interpretation of the tradition to be antitherapeutic at times when affirmative help is most needed.

Further, the mixed aspects of the tradition create allied problems in human sexuality with which the pastoral counselor must deal. As recipient, bearer, and product of the tradition, both in its affirmative and negative aspects, the pastoral counselor needs to be aware of his own sexuality and the manner in which it affects his counseling. Without such insight, the pastor is at the mercy of unexamined feelings and rationalizing defenses which are counterproductive in working with people. In addition, other concerns in human sexuality become evident to the pastor, such as the changing role of women and the sexuality of single persons in a world oriented around married couples.

Finally, the pastoral counselor works within, and is officially related to, an institution, the church, whose official bodies and individual members make interpretations of the mixed tradition of human sexuality. Because of these interpretations, the pastoral counselor encounters confusion between the roles he seeks to fulfill and conflict about what is expected of him by those with whom he works and whom he may be called on to counsel. And these confused and conflicting expectations can hinder the therapeutic thrust of his counseling.

The Tradition and Sexual Expression

When Mr. and Mrs. Jones come to see the pastor, the presenting situation revolves around Mrs. Jones's statement: "No matter how hard I try to understand, I just can't respond to him. Somehow it just seems wrong and I can't do it." What Mrs. Jones "can't do" is obvious enough: she cannot respond to her husband sexually in a manner which is satisfactory to both of them. Why she cannot respond becomes clearer as she explains.

Mrs. Jones: Please understand— I do love my husband very much—that has nothing to do with it. In fact, loving him so much is what brings me here to talk about it. But . . . well, I just wasn't raised that way . . . .

Pastor: You weren't raised that way . . . you mean, to be able to . . . .

Mrs. Jones: To be able to . . . to feel free enough when it comes to sex to show . . . to let Jim know that I love him.

Pastor: So that something in the way you were raised blocks you from responding.

Mrs. Jones: Yes, that's it. My parents never said too much about it, but they made it very clear that sex wasn't a subject for girls. And then

when I went to Sunday school, we were told stories about David and
. . . that woman on the roof, and Hosea's wife and others. And well,
you add that to barnyard talk and . . . I just can't respond. It seems
wrong and dirty.

Mrs. Jones is speaking out of a type of biblical tradition that
views sexual expression in a prohibitive and repressive manner.
While the full expression of the Christian tradition is mixed, con-
taining both affirmative and negative attitudes, the prominent
motif in both culture and tradition tends to be negative. Tragi-
cally, for someone enmeshed in such a problem, the affirmative
elements in the tradition concerning sex and marriage are either
ignored or not grasped until long after the years of childhood and
adolescence. By that time, the emotional context of such learning
is so well established that it is difficult to overcome it simply by
introducing new knowledge about biblical affirmations of sex. So
the pastor faces the difficult task of translating a biblical heritage
which, in itself, has been productive of the problem.[1]

The pastor, as he hears Mrs. Jones, discovers that he himself is
not immune to the problem she presents, for he recalls with distress his conversation of the night before with his own wife.
Unfortunately, while his intellectual training has enabled him to
recognize the mixed nature of the heritage of sex, there has been
little in his theological education which has aided him in coming
to grips with his own sexuality and the emotions which it produces. Thus he may attempt in his counseling either to keep the
subject of sex at the purely intellectual level, or, as in the case of
the pastoral counselors described by Masters and Johnson, to
avoid discussing it altogether, or, when the subject is raised, to

1. "In essence, when an individual's sexual value system has no positive connotation, how little the chance for truly effective sexual expression. The fact that most
men and women survive the handicap of strict religious orthodoxy to function
with some semblance of sexual effectiveness does not mean that these men and
women are truly equipped to enjoy the uninhibited freedom of sexual exchange.
Their physical response patterns, developing in spite of their orthodox religious
negation of an honorable role for sexual function, are immature, constrained, and,
at times, even furtive." William H. Masters and Virginia E. Johnson, *Human
Sexual Inadequacy* (Boston: Little, Brown and Co., 1970), p. 179.

"belittle the importance of the sexual problem."[2] The affirmative aspects of the Christian tradition in sex thus tend to be overwhelmed by the emotional impact of the negative.

Changing Roles for Women

Mrs. Brown's desire to work outside the home reflects a situation that is becoming increasingly pressing in today's world. Although magazines and books debate the issue every month, the pastor is suddenly called upon to face this new dimension in human sexuality in his counseling.

Mrs. Brown, in a thoughtful and sober way, attempts to explain to him her feelings as a person who finds the role expected of her as a woman both restricting and limiting.

"I do so much want to get back into social work where I can be alive and grow again."

But she is aware of, and sensitive to, her husband's opposition to this change.

"Alan was raised differently and he has a different picture of me as a wife and mother. He loves me and he wants to help me, but . . . well . . . not this far."

And then Mrs. Brown asks the questions which bring her to her pastor: "Am I wrong? Is it my Christian duty to stay home with the children? What does God expect of me and my life?"

Preparing a response, the pastor recalls that his own wife talked about being forced into some stereotypes she did not choose and does not enjoy. Yet she *did* stay home with their children as his mother had done with him. But times seem to be changing and women, "Well—what do they want? What about them?" he thinks.

The pastor knows that early Christianity, in its concern to

---

2. Ibid., p. 178. "Trained by theological demand to uninformed immaturity in matters of sexual connotation, both marital partners had no concept of how to cope when their sexual dysfunction was manifest. Their first approach to professional support was to agree to seek pastoral counseling. Here their individual counselors were as handicapped by orthodoxy as were their supplicants."

avoid the sexual excesses and immorality of surrounding cultures, gave promise of becoming a liberating force for women in the ancient world. But he is also aware that the subsequent centuries have not seen that promise fulfilled. The contemporary church, as the institutional representative of Christianity, is often no more enlightened and frequently less enlightened than contemporary culture. Presenting a confusing picture, some denominations of the American church allow the ordination of women while others deny women any position of power within the administrative structure. Both the acceptance and the denial are given biblical and theological foundations, attesting again to the mixed character of the tradition.

One of the difficulties in working at the problem with Mrs. Brown is the fact that while the traditional model of a woman as wife, mother, and homemaker is endorsed in the biblical-theological tradition, there is little obvious reference to support her return to work. This adjustment for a new life style finds its main support in contemporary writings that have little reference to religion. Yet there is an affirmative thrust toward the development of personhood in the biblical-theological tradition, and this the pastor recognizes both in the tradition and in her question.

The question Mrs. Brown asks, "What does God expect of me?" is particularly difficult for the pastor. He feels, in turn, that he must ask the same question for Mr. Brown, who is unhappy with his wife's request. And if the pastor tries to answer the question, does he answer as God would have him do or as a member of the male sex? Can he, as a male pastor with a traditional family orientation, answer without bias? The pastor must wonder—and so must Mrs. Brown.

The pastor does the only thing he sees possible. Without giving an answer, he suggests a meeting with the two of them to talk over the problem. And as Mrs. Brown leaves, the pastor thinks it over again: Is there a base line in Christianity from which to translate the tradition for this new problem in human sexuality? Can Christianity speak to the new woman?

The Unmarried Couple

The young graduate students with their disarming manner and disturbing request sit and wait for the pastor to respond. To them, the request is the logical conclusion to an examination of the nature and meaning of marriage. While the state requires the issuing of a proper marriage license and its subsequent registration, it obviously asks none of the pertinent questions about the meaning of marriage. Legal registration of the event has no more meaning than the registration of political party affiliation. The meaning of marriage has to do rather with the decision of the couple concerning the nature of the relationship they wish to establish. By his participation as the representative of the church community, the pastor—and even he is not necessary for a marriage to occur—adds a particular religious definition to the relationship between the couple. So they make the request to the pastor that their marriage take place immediately and be publicly recognized, with the state license to follow in one year.

While the couple advance the logic of their request, the pastoral counselor enumerates to himself other factors which are not immediately apparent in their situation. Clearly, this young couple have met the tests of responsibility, concern, and love which he would ask of any couple planning marriage. At the same time, he is aware that in the Judaic tradition, betrothal was tantamount to marriage. Remembering that tradition, he wonders how he would have handled the situation if Joseph and Mary had come to him. Certainly the breakdown of meaning in legislative and prohibitive codes always occurs at the point of individual situations. Yet, does one exception make exceptions of all other such situations? A line must be established, the pastor thinks, but where —on the particular situation or on a legalistic statement?

The pastor recognizes also that the community or societal demands for a marriage include the legality of a state license at the time of marriage. This demand may be misplaced in the sense that it insists upon a type of respectability without asking the appropriate questions about the meaning of a marriage. But society will make its judgment and the couple will need to face and live with that judgment.

Then the pastor's thoughts turn to what role he should exercise in relation to their request. They appear to be asking him to participate as a representative of the church community and not as an individual. As an individual he may approve of their action, but does this individual approval grant him the right to act in the name of the community? This question becomes important, for example, if his church has made a formal statement against all sexual intercourse outside of marriage.

So the pastor muses on the broader question which comes to him through this couple's request. On what basis does the pastoral counselor deal with those who are on the periphery of church and community: the singles, the divorced, the widowed? Does marriage and its particular needs and standards set the pattern for people who are not married? Does human sexuality find meaning and expression only in marriage?

Pastoral Roles and Expectations

Mrs. Smith's distress over her son's masturbation highlights another dimension of the counseling pastor's complicated task.

"Pastor, what can I do to get him to stop?"

"Stop?" the pastor thinks. "As if I can stop all the thoughts that spring from an adolescent boy's growth!"

In the very words of her request the counselor hears a directive: "Masturbation is a bad habit which good boys don't get into. Therefore you, as a man concerned with the good, must help me to stop him." She has made her judgment and her expectancies are clear. The pastoral counselor, she feels, needs only to respond with a concrete suggestion for stopping her son's bad habit.

But what does the pastor do with other information which filters through his mind at this point? He is aware that masturbation among adolescent boys is almost universal. Further, there is no medical evidence to indicate that it is physically harmful; and

where harm does occur, it is a harm imposed not upon the body
but upon the mind of the boy by adults who mishandle the situation when they discover it. The pastor is also aware that attitudes
toward masturbation are affected by social class status, as are
attitudes toward premarital intercourse and other sexual practices, and that what is really involved is more a matter of prior
judgment—prejudice—than ethical decision.[3]

Yet Mrs. Smith's view of masturbation is undoubtedly held by
others within the congregation and her particular circle of friends.
The pastor realizes that if he follows the behavioral science
statements on masturbation he will be in direct conflict with Mrs.
Smith, and that his statements may then be interpreted as a
watershed for all his views on matters related to human sexuality.
If he could make his statement simply as a counselor, as a
psychologist-counselor does, the broader implications could be
avoided. Yet, while the pastor may see himself at that moment in
the role of counselor, he realizes that Mrs. Smith sees him as
pastor in a total sense. Whether he preaches, counsels, teaches,
or administers, he is, above all, her pastor. This diffusion of role
allows him no immunity; in the minds of those hearing him what
he says is not viewed in terms of the particular role in which he
says it. And this totality of role creates a very difficult situation
for the pastor encountering human sexuality, particularly when
the biblical-theological tradition is viewed as primarily negative
and prohibitive.

The pastor asks himself the big questions implicit in Mrs.
Smith's request: Must he repress information from the behavioral
sciences in problems of this type and speak only to individual
expectancies? Must he subordinate his role as counselor in order
to reduce the pressures which might devolve upon his other
roles? Dare he be prophetic in the role of pastoral counselor and
defy the expectancies of those who hear him? And where does
the prophetic stop and foolhardiness begin?

3. Alfred C. Kinsey, Wardell B. Pomeroy, and Clyde E. Martin, *Sexual Behavior
in the Human Male* (Philadelphia: W. B. Saunders Co., 1948), chap. 14.

The Task of Translation

As counselor the pastor faces a variety of difficulties in the area of human sexuality. Elements such as empathy, unconditional positive regard for the counselee, and the establishment of a good relationship are of course fundamental to all counseling. But the problems faced by the counseling pastor in the area of human sexuality are so filled with emotional and ethical overtones that they require far more than fundamental counseling skills alone.

Furthermore, it is apparent that the knowledge of human sexuality supplied by behavioral science cannot in itself meet the unique needs of the pastoral counselor. Such knowledge is of course essential, as is skill in using it. But for effective counseling the pastor needs more than simply such knowledge and skill.

The pastoral counselor, above all, must deal with the biblical-theological tradition in which he stands. He must understand the nature of that tradition and he must personally come to grips with it. The pastor unwilling to do this concedes the distinctiveness of what he brings to every counseling situation.

But because the negative features of the biblical-theological heritage have become entrenched with the religious and cultural understandings of human sexuality, a basic skill of translation is required of the pastoral counselor in this area. To counter this negative aspect of the heritage, he needs to both understand and make explicit within his counseling situations the highly affirmative thrust within the tradition. By developing skill in translating the affirmations present in the tradition, the counselor will be enabled to bring the resources of this rich heritage to contemporary people in a way that helps them both in their attitudes and in their behavior.

2. The Tradition and Pastoral Counseling in Sexuality

Pastor Edwin Frost tapped last Sunday's bulletin against the palm of his left hand as he pondered the reactions to one of its announcements: "Next Sunday evening the pastor will begin a series with the youth group entitled 'The Christian and Sex.' " Even as he had written it he knew what would happen. Christians have always had difficulty with sex.

Mrs. Grant had hurried over to him immediately after the service to express her appreciation for his effort. "You know, young people really need to know where the church stands on sex. Teenagers today think they can do anything they want to with anybody."

Mr. Wright had stopped to speak his concern about whether sex was really the business of the church. "That's a subject best left to their parents."

The Farthings dropped in at the office and explained that the subject of sexual behavior was an area of great concern to them as parents. "It seems as though no one is holding the lines these days. Nobody seems to be talking about moral standards anymore. Everyone is so permissive. If the church doesn't teach these standards, where are the kids going to learn them?" Mr. Farthing said vehemently.

Later in the day, Mrs. Driver phoned to tell him how worried she was. "I'm sure you mean well," she said, "but I really think you'd do better to spend more time on 'the Christian' and less time on sex. Young people are so suggestible. I'm afraid with your program they'll just get all worked up and the first thing you know one of our girls will be in trouble. As far as I'm concerned, the less said, the better."

Mulling over their comments, Pastor Frost speculated about the reasons for the stir among his members. For Mrs. Driver, the subject of sex is too threatening even to be discussed. Mr. Wright feels that sex is inappropriate for the church to teach. Both share the opinion that the subject of sex is best ignored, because it has no real part in the Christian life. Mrs. Grant and the Farthings take an opposite point of view. Sex is too powerful and potentially dangerous to be ignored. They want heavy controls and a strict moral code, and for these they look to the church.

The pastor muses to himself: "Are silence or prohibitive moralism the only two stances the church can take in its effort to communicate values in human sexuality? Has the Christian faith nothing to say about such a vital part of life except: Don't mention it, and don't do it unless you are married? What a far cry from the spirit in which Jesus lived and taught! What a contrast to the Hebrew's affirmation that sex was part of God's good creation, to be used rightly and enjoyed! Yet there's no escaping the fact that Christianity today, as it is understood by many people, is antisexual."

Gary and Allison Simms come to mind. They are a couple with whom Pastor Frost has been counseling. Gary brought the problem to him first.

Gary: Look, I know I'm not a member of your church, or any church for that matter. But my wife is, and that's what I want to talk about. I didn't think—before we were married, that is—that our religious differences would matter much, but now they seem enormous. But my wife has changed from a generous, unselfish, easy to get along with person to a—well, I don't know what to call her. I can just tell you that her moral standards—her Christian ideals, as she calls them—are really getting to me. Why we haven't even been married a year, and she's already on my back about my drinking . . . as if one drink before dinner was going to make an alcoholic of me. And she nags me about coming to church with her on Sundays. I guess I might be able to ride with those if sex was OK. But she is really a prude.

Pastor: It sounds like you are having a rough first year!

Gary: I never expected anything like this. I thought at first that she was just inexperienced or shy and that was all right. I thought after a couple of months she would come around and find out what a great experience sex is. I even picked up some books for her, explaining different techniques and things. Was that ever a mistake! She was furious.

Pastor: Why do you think the books angered her?

Gary: You tell me! I know what she said, but I'm still baffled. She said the books were dirty, that I must think very little of her to bring home that kind of pornography. Gees! The books had a few pictures of different positions, but the whole purpose was to help her. As it is, neither one of us gets anything out of sex. She's as stiff as a board, and who likes to make love to a board? I'm at an impasse, in more ways than one.

Pastor: You feel, then, that Allison's feelings about sex have something to do with her ideas about Christianity.

Gary: I'm sure of it. She told me that if I were a Christian I'd understand. And if I didn't drink I wouldn't want sex all the time. All the time—that gets me. Why she acts as if it's dirty and wrong for me to want something more than a quick, once a week, one position routine. She says, "After all, it's not like we're trying to have a baby." Well, at this point, I'm even ready for that if it would be any improvement, but she has a job. And anyway I don't really think that would work, because basically she thinks sex is wrong if you do it for pleasure. And I think she's dead wrong and so are the rest of you Christians. Sex is what marriage is all about. It's the ultimate pleasure a man and woman can have. I know, from past experience. And I think there are plenty of people who would agree with me.

The conversation was disturbing, Pastor Frost recalled, because Gary Simms's comments about Christian devaluation of sex came uncomfortably close to the truth. And suddenly the question was haunting him again as he reviewed the comments his own congregation had made. How did we come to this near denial of sexuality, given a Hebraic heritage which chose the symbol of sexual union to describe the knowing, caring character of Yahweh's relationship to his people?

Pastor Frost's question pinpoints a unique problem in the Christian tradition, for the biblical and theological writings contain a curious mixture of attitudes about human sexuality. The thrust of the biblical tradition is affirmative while the overall view in the historical-theological tradition is heavily negative.

The Old Testament

The Old Testament writings value sexuality as part of God's good creation, to be used rightly and enjoyed. In fact, sex played a significant part in Hebrew life; for man, created in the image of God, was given both the capacity and the responsibility for procreation. And since the Hebrew held no doctrine of personal immortality, he came to look upon his progeny, born of his seed, as an extension of himself. Coupled with this was his conviction that Yahweh had chosen the Hebrew people for a special destiny. Family lines, then, were quite important to him, and the religious laws and cultural mores of sexual behavior reflected a concern to keep those lines clarified. But no denial or repression of sexuality was indicated for the Hebrew male.

There is present, however, in the Old Testament writings, a double standard of sexual ethics. Deuteronomic laws stressed female virginity before marriage and fidelity following marriage, but there were no such statutes for Hebrew men. This double standard grew out of the Hebraic understanding of reproduction. Unaware of the existence of the ovum, the Hebrews thought that the man alone carried the seed for new life, while the woman contributed merely the place in which that seed could grow and be protected. Human reproduction was not unlike planting a seed in the ground. Consequently, male sexuality centered on the ability and responsibility of the man for planting his seed. The Hebrew man had freedom and access to any woman, so long as she was not the property of another man, and any child that resulted was legitimately his. In comparison, female sexuality was viewed as inferior since the woman contributed nothing substantial of herself to the new life. Her biological role in reproduction and her social position as property of a father, husband, or master gave the Hebrew woman a peculiar status. As the bearer of progeny in a family line, her virginity and sexual fidelity became matters of community concern. Codes of sexual behavior evolved to protect her chastity and thus ensure that family lines be kept pure. And even though female sexual activity was highly controlled, the restrictions were without the repressive and negativistic overtones that characterize later Christian writings.

Jesus

We have no teaching of Jesus about sexuality as such, though he certainly stood firmly within the Hebraic tradition. Although he was sharply critical of the religious legalism in which that tradition had become entangled, we can safely assume that he had no arguments with the affirmative Hebraic evaluation of sex. Moreover, the Gospels provide important emphases indicating values of human life which give positive meaning to sexuality.[1] These emphases become important in evaluating later negative developments in the Christian view of sex.

Jesus viewed man holistically, as a unity. This is in contrast to later Christian anthropology which described man as spirit encumbered by a sinful body.

Jesus criticized a legalistic approach to right living which stressed observable behavior and virtually ignored personal attitudes and intentions. In both parable and encounter, Jesus called attention to motivation. He asked about the meaning of the act, as illustrated by his remarks concerning the Pharisee and the publican who prayed at the temple. Jesus taught that conformity to the law counts for little if it is not backed by integrity of spirit.

In Jesus' mind, the intent of the Mosaic law could be stated in the commandment to love God with all one's being and to love one's neighbor as oneself. That love included respect, understanding, acceptance, compassion, forgiveness, and giving of self. The welfare of persons was more important than specific Judaic laws themselves.

Jesus met people in their unique situations with understanding and direction for movement. In his encounters with the rich young ruler, Zaccheus the tax collector, Mary of Magdalene, and

1. Seward Hiltner deals with this thesis at some length in *Sex Ethics and the Kinsey Reports* (New York: Association Press, 1953). See also William G. Cole, *Sex in Christianity and Psychoanalysis* (New York: Oxford University Press, 1955).

others, he was concerned with their movement toward wholeness of life.

Jesus' life style puzzled those who expected him to follow in the ascetic pattern of John the Baptist. It disturbed some that Jesus ate and drank in celebration (weddings included) and enjoyed the company of many kinds of people. In contrast to later Christians, he in no way denied either earthly life or sexuality.

Among the few words about sex attributed to Jesus were these: "You have learned that they were told, 'Do not commit adultery' but what I tell you is this: If a man looks on a woman with a lustful eye, he has already committed adultery with her in his heart" (Matt. 5:28). This quotation has frequently been used to support the belief that Jesus condemned all sexual desire. But as William Cole and others have indicated, this reading misses Jesus' point of criticism against a legalistic approach to right conduct.[2] His point was not to deny sexuality as a good gift of God, but to illustrate that a legalistic interpretation of the law against adultery does not fulfill its intention to guard against the misuse of persons. In effect he is saying, "You congratulate yourselves on your good behavior and technically you are within the limits of the law, but your attitude is not in harmony with its spirit." His remarks seem to be more an insistence that sexuality cannot be reduced to the act of intercourse and that it is to be enjoyed rightly.

In short, Jesus viewed the person in totality and sexuality was part of that totality. He taught that life was to be enjoyed in right relationship to God and to neighbor. This right relationship is found in the acknowledgment of personhood under God, and is expressed in loving, caring, and responsible living. Sexuality, then, as an aspect of personhood, falls under that rubric.

Paul

The door to a negative interpretation of sex was opened by the Pauline writings. Certain of Paul's comments were understood

2. Cole, *Sex in Christianity*, p. 16.

by later Christians to mean that sex was a hindrance to the spiritual life:

> It is a good thing for a man to have nothing to do with women.
>
> (1 Cor. 7:1)
>
> To the unmarried and to widows I say this: it is a good thing if they stay as I am myself; but if they cannot control themselves, they should marry. Better be married than burn with vain desire.
>
> (1 Cor. 7:8)

Yet Paul himself informs us of the context in which his remarks were made:

> What I mean, my friends, is this. The time we live in will not last long. While it lasts, married men should be as if they had no wives; mourners should be as if they had nothing to grieve them, the joyful as if they did not rejoice. . . . For the whole frame of this world is passing away.
>
> (1 Cor. 7:29–31)

Furthermore, he takes care to separate his own opinion from the commands he understands to be from the Lord:

> To the rest I say this, as my own word, not as the Lord's . . . .
>
> (1 Cor. 7:12)
>
> I have no instructions from the Lord, but I give my judgement as one who by God's mercy is fit to be trusted.
>
> (1 Cor. 7:25)

It is inappropriate, then, to derive general rules for life (as later Christians did in interpreting Paul) from these particularized comments spoken for a time of stress. As David Mace has said, "It is like quoting instructions issued to citizens by a wise and capable mayor at the time of an impending air raid as a basis for civic policy after the war is over."[3]

---

3. David R. Mace, *The Christian Response to the Sexual Revolution* (Nashville: Abingdon Press, 1970), pp. 36–37.

Furthermore, we cannot overlook Paul's remarks about the nature of loving between husband and wife, nor the fact that he chose the marriage union as symbol for the relationship of Christ and the church.

> Thus it is that (in the words of Scripture) "a man shall leave his father and mother and shall be joined to his wife, and the two shall become one flesh." It is a great truth that is hidden here. I for my part refer it to Christ and to the church, but it applies also individually: each of you must love his wife as his very self; and the woman must see to it that she pays her husband all respect.
>
> (Eph. 5:30–33)

Fundamentally, then, the biblical tradition looks at sexuality affirmatively, as part of life that has meaning and value when it is experienced in an unexploitive fashion. Its high symbolic worth was recognized by both Old and New Testament writers.

The History of Theology

The historical-theological tradition of Christianity presents an altogether different picture of sexuality. Even as early as the latter part of the first century, sexuality began to feel the influence of Hellenistic dualism. And under the growing dominance of dualistic thought, the Christian attitude toward sexuality began its deviation from the biblical tradition. Dualism viewed the drama of life as a contest between the world of the spirit, essentially good and pure, and the world of matter, contaminated by evil. As this philosophy was in varying degrees assimilated into Christian thought, life came to be viewed as a pilgrimage of struggle, precipitated by Adam's fall, in which the spirit of man sought to overcome or control the temptations of the flesh. And sexuality, as an expression of the flesh, was considered sinful and contaminated.

Augustine exercised the single most important influence on later Christian thinking about sexuality. His views prevailed basically unchanged throughout the medieval and reformation periods; they still hold an attraction for Christians today. Although Augustine fervently argued against dualism in his writings, he nonetheless allowed its influence in the area of sexuality to remain unexorcised. His negativism was provoked in part by his own lifelong struggle with sexuality. His conversion to Christianity, described in his *Confessions,* represents a long-sought victory over the plague of sexual desire. In Augustine's mind, the Fall resulted in a state of general concupiscence (insatiability) for man which had marked effects on sexuality. Where sexual expression before the Fall would have been rational, contemplative, and for the sole purpose of procreation, since the Fall it has been spoiled by lust, passion, and uncontrollability. Thus the highest goal for the Christian was the state of celibacy or virginity. Marriage, while acknowledged as good because Augustine thought it to be divinely instituted, nevertheless was described as "the remedy for sinful lust" and as "medicine for immorality." He believed that all sexual expression aside from procreative purpose was sinful. Even here, he proposed the idea that sexual desire was responsible for the transmission of original sin from parent to child. Augustine was convinced that celibacy was better in the eyes of God than any marital intercourse, however loving it might be.

Sexuality, for Augustine and other Christian thinkers who followed him, was potentially dangerous. The drive for sexual intercourse was seen as an expression of man's sinful nature. The reformers, Luther and Calvin, questioned the view that celibacy was a higher state than marriage, but they continued to share Augustine's belief that the sexual life of man had been contaminated by the Fall. Both reformers married, insisting that marriage was ordained by God, but still they regarded marriage as a necessary remedy for controlling lust. Strangely enough, Calvin was less pessimistic than Luther about sex. While Luther was impressed with the raging power of lust, Calvin thought that it could be controlled and used constructively. But his attempts to specify how it should be controlled led him into a legalism which prohibited all but passionless, moderate intercourse in marriage for the purposes of procreation. Outside of intercourse in marriage, sex was sinful, and Calvin thought the Old Testament was quite fair in prescribing the death penalty for adultery and sodomy. So the reformation passed and still no positive view of human sexuality had surfaced. Negativism continued to color sexual attitudes in the centuries that followed. In America, the New England puritans exacerbated that negativism in their attempt to live the sanctified life. Pleasure and beauty as temptations to sin were viewed with grave suspicion. And sexuality, to the extent that it was enjoyable, was met with repression and condemnation.

Contemporary Traditions

Today, far into the twentieth century, the Christian church still operates under the enduring influence of dualism. Even though it has recovered much of the life-world affirmation present in the Old Testament and Gospel writings, as evidenced by its concern for ecology and for social amelioration, the church's antisexual bias is still strong. By and large it continues to ignore sexuality as a part of life or to stave it off with prohibitions and restraints. Under the tidal wave of cultural preoccupation with sex, this stance becomes increasingly difficult to maintain. Furthermore, it offers little help to the Christian in developing guidelines which can give meaning and value to sexual expression in his own life. Anxieties rise and he senses his inadequacy to understand the sexual revolution taking place around him.

Pastor Frost's announcement brought these anxieties to the surface. Silence and prohibition only perpetuate antisexual attitudes. Even more important, such treatment evades the responsibility of affirming the values of human living which Jesus lived and taught—values which give sexual expression its meaning and enriching power.

But Gary Simms's conversation was disturbing to the pastor for another reason. For while Simms voiced some legitimate criticisms about Christian negativism, his own mechanical approach to sexual pleasure seemed devoid of personal love and caring. In his own way, Gary Simms was expressing the new puritanism. And Pastor Frost almost pulled out Rollo May's book from the shelf in front of him.[4] The situation, he thought, would be humorous if it weren't such a sad commentary on the times—Gary Simms, the new puritan, distressed with the old puritanism of his wife. For just as the old puritan tends to separate sex from life by denying it any positive value, the new puritan separates sexual pleasure from total life involvement by viewing sex as a mechanical, physiological sensation. Simms actually hoped that with a few good books and a variety of positions and techniques, he would reach his goal of good sex as the ultimate experience between a man and a woman.

Simms's remarks were well founded when he observed that many others shared his views. For our contemporary culture is eroticized to the point where sex is an obsessive theme. Popular literature, films, and songs tantalize the imagination with fantasies which picture sex as salvation, excitement, the ultimate experience. Advertising capitalizes on fantasy by using "sex appeal" as the bait for buyers of everything from toothpaste and cars to bathroom bowl cleaner. Sexual pleasure is dangled before people as an end in itself, with a market inundated by books promising to "tell all" about "how to."

This contemporary preoccupation with sexual pleasure needs to be criticized for its diminution of sexuality to a form of physical-psychological sensation alone, and for its failure to understand the sexual relationship as an expression of love between two people. At the same time, this reduction appears to bring problems of its own. Clinical statistics indicate that more people are seeking professional help for sexual problems than ever before. Clinician Rollo May reports, "We are becoming used to the plaint from the couch or patient's chair that 'We made love, but I didn't feel anything.' "[5] Men and women want sexual pleasure without emotional involvement and then wonder why sex isn't any good. Masters and Johnson have indicated that

4. Rollo May, *Love and Will* (New York: W. W. Norton and Co., 1969).
5. Ibid., p. 59.

attitudes and expectations play a significant role in sexual dysfunction. They discovered in clinical experience that excessive concern with sexual performance actually interferes with normal sexual functioning. The man who complains of impotence frequently looks upon coitus as a matter of performance on his part. He concentrates so intently on what he is doing, whether or not he is gaining an erection and whether or not he will be able to maintain erection long enough to satisfy his partner, that he defeats himself and is unable to "perform." And the dysfunctional woman who strives to achieve the desired orgasm becomes goal-oriented to the point where she becomes a mere spectator in the effort, rather than a participant in mutual pleasuring.[6]

Paradoxically, much of contemporary sexual expression is as inadequate and biased as is the negative expression in Christianity. In reducing sexuality to the experience of physiological sensation, it strips away enhancing power for human relationship.

Thus, the meetings for young people on "The Christian and Sex," as announced by Pastor Frost, become all the more urgent. For in a real sense, the pastor will be speaking to an impoverished group, to people made poor by the void of heavy silence from the church and by a culture's idolatry of sensual pleasure. Christians bear some responsibility in that deprivation. Caught in a cycle of anxiety and repression, they have often failed to appropriate the liberating message of the gospel as it gives meaning and substance to human sexual relationships. The Simmses need this liberating word as much as the adolescents do, for today many bring to marriage a seriously limited understanding of the sexual relationship. In his counseling, the pastor will need to communicate an appreciation of sexuality enriched by the spirit of the biblical tradition.

A Constructive View of Human Sexuality

Against the backdrop of an antisexual tradition within Christianity and of a culture's present absorption with erotic stimula-

---

6. William H. Masters and Virginia E. Johnson, *Human Sexual Inadequacy* (Boston: Little, Brown and Co., 1970), pp. 11–14.

tion, a viable and contemporary view of sexuality is urgently needed for pastoral counseling. Such a view must begin with the clearly affirmative thrust of biblical tradition that human sexuality is of God and intended to be experienced as an enhancement of human relationships.

In contrast to the negative tradition in Christianity which regarded sexuality as a problem controllable only by repression and prohibition, a constructive Christian view indicates that sexuality, as a part of life, has positive meaning and value. Without denying the need for guidelines and controls, it seeks to derive general principles of guidance which avoid legalism and reflect Christian values of personhood and relationship. As Seward Hiltner has said, ". . . the ordering of sex by society should be for the realization of personal and interpersonal values, *not for the sake of control as such.*"[7]

The biblical tradition does not spell out a theology of sex. But general principles can be derived from the tradition which afford a base line from which to deal with sexuality in contemporary life.

First, sexual intimacy when experienced within a responsible framework of commitment carries the potential for deepening and enriching relationships. Sexual expression which grows out of mutual caring brings self-disclosure and intimate knowing of another. This experience was valued by biblical writers significantly enough to stand as a metaphor for the God-man relationship. Paul called the church the bride of Christ, and Ezekiel and Hosea referred to Israel as the bride of Yahweh. "I will betroth you to myself for ever, betroth you in lawful wedlock with unfailing devotion and love; I will betroth you to myself to have and to hold, and you shall know the Lord" (Hos. 2:19). Remembering that the word "know" also connoted sexual intimacy, Hosea's statement becomes a powerful one. Knowing occurs in a relationship which is deeply personal, affectional, and with no separation between love and sex.[8]

7. Hiltner, *Kinsey Reports*, p. 177.
8. Joseph Blenkinsopp, *Sexuality and the Christian Tradition* (Dayton, Ohio: Pflaum Press, 1969), p. 38.

Second, sexual expression enhances human relationship when it is experienced in a personal unexploitive fashion. Jesus emphasized the value of the whole person, as a child of God and as one having the potential for growth and change. He further indicated that the meaning of life and personal fulfillment are found in the love of God and in caring human relationships. Facilitation of personal growth and loving relationships, then, can be understood as general goals for pastoral counseling. And these general goals operate as guidelines for sexual expression as well. In dealing with sexual matters, the pastor is concerned with such questions as these: What relational attitudes are present? What is the nature of sexual attitudes and activity? Is it exploitive? Does the sexual relationship enhance the total relationship? If not, why? The pastor utilizes the guidelines not to shame or condemn, but to inject relational meaning and personal value in a therapeutic way.

Finally, sexuality, as part of human experience, is dynamic and complex; at once biological urge, source of pleasuring, and self-expression. In the best sense, it combines responsible procreation, mutual pleasuring, and self-expression as a mode of communicating love for another. Like the rest of human experience it is not easily amenable to static codifications and legalisms, despite centuries of endeavor in that direction. The biblical writings have been misused on behalf of controlling and legalizing a minimal expression of sex, thus denying the tradition's own affirmation of a living God who is active in the history of his people. Biblical legalists, in their attempt to freeze bits of the tradition and subject sexuality to codification, have isolated themselves from sociological change and contemporary thought.

Combined with negativism toward sexuality, the result has been a formulation of irrelevant and, at times, absurd strictures. An excellent example of this type of legalism is the prohibition against masturbation, based on the biblical story of Onan. It is recorded in Genesis 38:8–11 that God was displeased with Onan for spilling his seed whenever he slept with Tamar, his dead brother's widow. The account needs to be understood in the context of a Hebrew culture which valued children as a heritage from the Lord, through whom the family name was continued. Onan violated the Levirate tradition which prevailed at the time by refusing to perpetuate his brother's name. But later interpreters have often taken this one sex act out of context and distorted and mythologized it, in spite of the fact that the practice of Levirate marriage has long since passed out of existence. Furthermore, there is the possibility that Onan's act was coitus interruptus rather than masturbation.

A contemporary approach to sexuality, then, while informed by the biblical tradition, must be open to changing patterns of life and reevaluation through the work of the Spirit.

Translating the Tradition

The task of translating a contemporary, affirmative Christian viewpoint toward sexuality in the counseling process is complex. Frequently, by the time a person seeks help in counseling, sexual attitudes are formed and integrated into his personality. These attitudes are invested with strong emotional content so that discussion alone is not sufficient. The pastoral counselor, therefore, cannot simply inform his counselee about a contemporary Christian viewpoint; he needs instead to translate that view cognitively, emotionally, and behaviorally.

Pastor Frost, counseling with Gary and Allison Simms, demonstrates a beginning effort in such a translation. The dialogue resumes the initial counseling session with Gary.

Pastor: You seem to be feeling a good deal of frustration and disappointment in your marriage . . . hoping for more sexual expression from Allison . . . and you think Christianity is the source of the trouble.

Gary: Yeah, I really think it is. She seems to think sex is unchristian.

Pastor: Well, a lot of Christians do seem to think that, and the Bible . . . are you familiar at all with the Bible?

Gary: No. Only what Allison quotes, and I don't think much of that!

Pastor: OK. But let's look at it a moment. The biblical writers . . . [continuation not quoted]

At this point, Frost decides to follow an educative form of counseling[9] by briefly explaining what happened to the Christian view of human sexuality over the centuries. Gary listens rather intently and says:

Gary: You surprise me. I expected you to be on Allison's side. . . . I sure wish you would talk to her.
Pastor: I don't really think I'm taking sides. I just wanted to get the record straight about Christianity and sex. But I do want to talk with Allison . . . and then I think all three of us should get together. OK?
Gary: Suits me. It can't get any worse . . . oh, I don't really mean that. But I'd like her to hear what you've just told me.

In this meeting, the pastor wanted to make known to Gary the story of Christianity and sex. Since Gary saw the sexual problem as fundamentally a cognitive issue (Allison's Christian views about sex are incorrect), Frost approached the problem at that level, using educative counseling. He was empathic and accepting to Gary, yet stated his case.

The next day, Allison came to see Pastor Frost. Their conversation, given here in briefed form, brought out her attitudes about Gary and the problem of sex. She began by explaining that the problem was one of religious differences.

Allison: We just have different sets of values. Gary sees life differently than I do.
Pastor: In the year you've been married, where do these differences come out most clearly?
Allison: Oh, in going to church. He won't go . . . and we have no spiritual life together . . . and then he drinks. And after two drinks, he gets ridiculous.
Pastor: And that makes you uncomfortable.
Allison: Yes, he always starts in on me.

(At this point, Pastor Frost discovers that Allison tries to avoid

9. Educative intervention and therapy is a method in which the counselor assumes the role of teacher. Such a style may entail supplying information, correcting mistakes, or pointing out new possibilities or directions. It is an active style of counseling but it does not use an authoritarian stance to force counselee acceptance. (Howard J. Clinebell, Jr., *Basic Types of Pastoral Counseling* [Nashville: Abingdon Press, 1966], chap. 2.)

saying how Gary starts in on her. He suspects she means sexual advances, but Allison still avoids answering. Finally, she admits she is referring to sex, but feels embarrassed to talk about it. The pastor carefully talks to her about it being important and she agrees to discuss it.)[10]

Allison: We're really not planning any children right now, so there's not much point in sex for me. And yet, I know that a man . . . needs release, shall we say . . . and I want to do my duty by Gary. But not so often. . . .

Pastor: So you find that he demands . . . or wants . . . too much from you. . . .

Allison: Yes, I do. It seems . . . any touch ends up in sex. When he kisses me, he wants sex . . . and he wants to do different things; he even gave me books. . . .

Pastor: And it keeps a pressure on you. And . . . well, the connection of love and sex always seems to go one way.

Allison: Love and sex? I can't think of a time when I feel less loved by Gary. He says he wants to give me pleasure, but real pleasure would be if he just left me alone.

The session closed with Pastor Frost puzzling out what had happened. Allison had expressed strong negative views about sex, but always in reaction to her husband's attitude. She had said nothing about how Christianity affected her viewpoint. Did she take this for granted since she was speaking to the pastor?

A subsequent session with Allison revealed that her reaction to sex was twofold: her education in the negative biblical-theological tradition made her see sex as something less than Christian; and, Gary's approach was so openly sexual and lacking in love, as she interpreted it, that she balked at sexual expression in any form. The pastor spent time, as he had with Gary, going over the history of Christianity and sex. Allison was puzzled and asked a number of questions. She seemed quite thought-

10. It is important for the pastor to be sensitive to embarrassment or reticence on the part of his counselee without glossing over or ignoring sexual material. Avoidance by the pastor serves only to confirm the belief that sex ought not to be talked about. The pastor can say openly that he senses this to be a difficult area for his counselee and demonstrate in his own discussion that sexual matters can be looked at sensitively and without embarrassment.

ful as she left, agreeing to return the next week with her husband.
The joint session began with the pastor:

Pastor: Thank you for coming. Before we begin, I want to review a bit as
to where I think we are.
    Gary, you came to the marriage with a tradition about sex; one
learned from our contemporary culture. And it's good in its own
way—open, enlightened, honest. But it has a flaw, and we'll talk
about that in a moment.
    Allison, you came to the marriage also with a tradition about sex;
one learned from a negative, biblical-theological approach. And it has
its values too—keeping things under careful control, discipline, and I
guess, a kind of piety. But *it* has a flaw. And we'll talk about that too.
    And I, as a pastor, also represent a tradition about sex. It's biblical
and it's Christian—most important, it's affirmative. Let me state three
things which it says:
First: sex has the possibility for deepening and enriching relationships.
Second: sex enhances human relationship when it is experienced
    in a personal, unexploitive fashion.
Third: sex is dynamic and complex, and that means it changes as we
    change. It is not just specific genital contacts, nor biological drive,
    but includes the meaning and value sexual behaviors have to indi-
    viduals and to their community.
Now, looking at these ideas about sexuality, let's examine the tradi-
tions *you* bring to them.

    At this point, there was a long silence and then both Allison
and Gary began to talk at once. Pastor Frost slowed down their
reactions and began to take them point by point.
    Had sex enriched and deepened their relationship? No, it had
not. Gary had never approached sex from that viewpoint (the
flaw of his tradition). Allison had rejected sex without seeing it as
an intimate part of enriching relationship (the flaw of her tradition). Frost suggested again that sex could be an enhancement
only after a relationship of mutuality had been established. Before that, it would continue to be a problem. This they agreed to
discuss further.
    But for sex to enrich relationship it had to avoid exploitation.
Perhaps Gary was more at fault here. He did not accept Allison

as she was, and in varying ways demanded change from her in order to meet his expectations and needs.

Finally, sex is a dynamic complex of physiological, psychological, and emotional aspects. Gary and Allison needed to see it as something fluid and dynamic rather than a static matter of "pleasure" or "duty." Sex could vary in expression and intensity. It could even have different phases within the same person at varying times. When misunderstood and misused, it could become dehumanizing and ugly; within a loving relationship, acceptance and understanding could surround it to make it an experience of joy and grateful self-giving.

Most important, this approach to sexuality had its roots in an affirmative biblical-theological tradition which both Gary and Allison could accept. Indeed, even more crucial, they now saw the need for precisely this perspective in their marriage.

Counseling Skills and Translation

In dealing with the Simmses, the Pastor had exercised varying basic skills of counseling: empathy, unconditional positive regard, support, interpretation, and educative intervention. But he was fully aware of the fact that change of attitude and viewpoint is a difficult and slow process. Frequently, insight alone is not sufficient to bring about lasting attitude change. Since thinking, feeling, and acting are not separate processes but interact with one another, Pastor Frost chose to deal with behavioral aspects as well.[11]

Specific homework assignments were designed to engage the Simmses in good interpersonal behavior. Appreciation and concern were to be shown in daily activity. They were asked to read a small paperback by David Mace, *Sexual Difficulties in Marriage*[12]; in discussion of the reading, they were encouraged to

---

11. Behavior therapy is a term descriptive of a number of counseling procedures which emphasize the learning of new behavior and the extinction of inappropriate behavior in present use by the counselee. (Arnold A. Lazarus, *Behavior Therapy and Beyond* [New York: McGraw-Hill, 1971].)

12. David R. Mace, *Sexual Difficulties in Marriage* (Philadelphia: Fortress Press, 1972).

share reactions openly and to listen with a view to understanding each other.

To break a negative response pattern for Allison, it was suggested that they both try for awhile to cut the tie between affectionate behavior and explicit sexual behavior, such as intercourse. This suggestion was intended to allow Allison to respond more freely to affection from Gary without the consequence of intercourse. At the same time, it would allow her to move toward Gary in an affectional way. Here Frost was following a technique used successfully by Masters and Johnson.[13]

Where the counselee shows strong and persistent fear or anxiety about sex, it may be necessary for the pastor to make referral.[14] Or, if he has had training in behavioral techniques, he may want to introduce systematic desensitization.[15] A proper use of desensitization, however, would warrant careful delineation of the problem in terms of specific points of fear or anxiety.

Counseling with the Simmses is by no means finished at this point. But enough has been said to indicate a functional or workable approach by the counseling pastor to some specific problems in human sexuality as he attempts translation of a contemporary Christian viewpoint. This approach avoids both the strong prohibitive stance familiar to the Christian tradition, and the permissive, laissez faire orientation of the culture. Guidelines are given for sexual attitude and behavior which are informed both by Christian values and the behavioral sciences.

Good counseling skills are important for this translation if the counselor is to facilitate needed attitude and behavior change. Cognizance must be taken of the whole person, and of the interrelation between thought, feeling, and behavioral expression. Principles of learning and development are important to the counsel-

13. Masters and Johnson, *Inadequacy*, pp. 60–83.
14. William B. Oglesby, Jr., *Referral in Pastoral Counseling* (Philadelphia: Fortress Press, 1969).
15. Systematic desensitization entails the presentation of anxiety-provoking situations in imagery form by the counselor to the counselee who has been taught to relax and to remain so during the presentation. (Robert R. Carkhuff, *Helping and Human Relations*, vol. 1 [New York: Holt, Rinehart and Winston, 1969], pp. 271–90.)

ing process as they aid the pastor in understanding the formation of sexual attitudes and patterns of interpersonal behavior, and in working with his counselees toward desired change and growth. The pastor, then, increases his effectiveness in counseling in the area of human sexuality as he practices these skills of bringing Christian meaning and value to the lives of his counselees.

3. The Pastor's Own Sexuality

When Pastor Carter pressed the doorbell at the home of a friend and fellow pastor, he wasn't very sure of himself. In fact, he was afraid. Maybe that's the way people always feel when they come for help, he thought. But now it was he who needed help—real help—and the feeling was unfamiliar and distinctly unpleasant.

The incident which took him to his friend's home had happened two nights before. He had gone to his office at the church to get a book when the phone rang. Answering, he heard a pleasant but troubled female voice ask if she could see him soon, preferably that very evening. She gave her name, which he didn't recognize, and in answer to his question said that it was a personal matter which she couldn't discuss over the phone. He agreed to a time, called his home to say he would be delayed, and sat down to read and wait.

When Betty Wilson arrived, she proved to be an attractive single person in her late twenties. Not a member of Carter's church, she talked a bit, thanked him for seeing her so soon and then began to explain her problem. In a sense, to Carter, the problem was fairly routine: she was having a personality clash with the young woman who shared her apartment and she needed help in analyzing their relationship and what the future might be. After an hour's conversation they agreed to meet again and Betty Wilson left.

Yet it was this one-hour meeting which was now taking Carter to his friend for consultation. After preliminary talk, the following dialogue took place:

Pastor Miller: OK. She came to your office and started to talk and then what?

Carter: Well, the first thing I noticed was that I started drifting away from what she was saying . . . I found myself more interested in her than in her problem.

Miller: I guess that can happen. So you got interested in her and . . . .
Carter: Yeah . . . and, Jim, to be honest, I found her darned attractive.
Now don't misunderstand . . . it wasn't anything she did; she wasn't
seductive or dressed that way or anything. But . . . I don't know . . . it
was the strangest feeling but she really attracted me.
Miller: Attracted you . . . in what sense?
Carter: I hate to admit it, but she . . . well, she attracted me sexually.
She really did. And while I was very careful and didn't say or do
anything to let her know how I felt, I did make an appointment to see
her again next week . . . and it really wasn't necessary.
Miller: An appointment next week?
Carter: Yes . . . and that just floors me. I just can't understand myself.
There's no need for me to act that way . . . and it scares me. I can't
understand what happened to me. And I called her to cancel the appointment but she wasn't home so . . . but, you know, I was almost
glad she wasn't home, because I'd like to see her again. But . . . Jim I
can't get involved like this . . . and I just can't understand it.
Miller: This *is* sticky for you and . . . uh . . . that appointment next week
is a problem. Bill . . . perhaps we should talk about other ways of
handling that . . . and, of course, helping her.

The Impact of the Sexual

The power of sex is awesome. To know that we are sexual
beings is one thing, but to discover the strength of that sexuality
can be overwhelming. So overwhelming and so anxiety-
producing is this strength that both Carter and Miller are having
trouble coming to grips with it.

Carter's experience is akin to that of the adolescent who feels
for the first time the sudden surge of sexuality. The ordered
boyhood—and girlhood—blend of body and mind, forged in
childhood, is overpowered and thrown into confusion. Most disturbing, this surge of sexuality has the thrust of an instinctual
mechanism that seems to have an autonomous existence. The
adolescent is plunged, as Erik Erikson explains, into a struggle
for a new and mature identity.[1] And the threat of identity diffu-

1. Identity is "a feeling of being at home in one's body, a sense of 'knowing where
one is going,' and an inner assuredness of anticipated recognition from those who
count" (p. 165). Identity diffusion is a condition of disintegration in the struggle
for identity and maturity. (Erik H. Erikson, *Identity: Youth and Crisis* [New
York: W. W. Norton and Co., 1968].)

sion is the same for Carter at this moment as it is for the adolescent.

The threat of diffusion would have been removed if Ms. Wilson had followed the stereotype of the seductive female asking the male counselor for help. Then the source of sexual stimulation would have been outside Carter and he would be relieved of responsibility for starting it. Furthermore, she would have been following a pattern familiar to his training. The folklore of counseling warns against seeing women in lonely offices at night and avoiding late evening visits to their homes. When Ms. Wilson called that evening, Carter was alert to possible hazards. But Betty Wilson did not play the role of female predator with the expectant male. She had a problem, she discussed it, and she went home. The only untoward factor in the counseling session was Carter's own sexual feeling about her; it was this irrational breach of his ordered life which confounded him.

Pastor Miller, as Carter's friend and now his counselor, is having difficulty coming to grips with the problem. Obviously aware of the sexual situation, he attempts to handle it by shutting it off in the future: don't see her again. But Carter will not ignore the problem and the dialogue continues:

Carter: Sure that appointment is a problem. But that's not my concern right now. Look, Jim—what do I do about the way I feel? I've never felt this way before—at least, not since college, and certainly not since I married Marge. But in college it was different. I'm supposed to be in control now.

Miller: All right, let's look at it. To be honest, your situation and your feelings about it scare me more than I want to admit. I've had the same experience myself that you had—and I guess I've been lucky that nothing ever came of it. So maybe that's the point at which to start. You felt that way about . . . uh . . . Betty, but so far you've done nothing except to feel it; and that makes a big difference.

Carter: But I *did* think it—and I still feel it, God help me! And that's just as bad. You remember what Jesus said about looking at a woman with lust . . . I feel guilty as hell!

The Unique Stance of the Pastoral Counselor

The distinctive stance of the pastoral counselor is clearly visible in this section of the dialogue. Psychological and psychiatric counselors would at this point bring to the counseling scene their particular educational background in the behavioral sciences and medical arts. The counseling pastor, however, in addition to at least some knowledge of these disciplines, now adds his special training in biblical and theological thought. Yet this particular training is not something just added on to the other knowledges; rather, it serves primarily as the grid through which all the other information is filtered. Such use of the biblical-theological materials is the distinctive mark of the pastoral counselor.[2] Furthermore, in the pastoral counselor this biblical-theological material is not only a matter of basic knowledge but also the source of his faith, and hence of his worldview. The emotional investment, therefore, becomes extraordinary at this point, for the grid is both faith and life for the pastor. So the nature of the grid—the biblical-theological understanding—determines the viewpoint of the pastoral counselor. But in the area of human sexuality much of the biblical-theological material is negative and restrictive; unless clarified, it often serves to constrict the approaches to a counselee's problem.

Carter and Miller are at such a point when they engage in the question: What is the relationship between a thought and an act? Carter quotes the words of Jesus in which looking at a woman with a lustful eye is tantamount to commiting adultery with her in one's heart (Matt. 5:28). If taken at face value, Carter is correct in condemning himself. But, also taken at face value, the statement does not represent a correct evaluation of Jesus' attitude on this matter. So Miller responds:

Miller: Now wait a minute, Bill. You're building a case against yourself on the basis of Jesus' statement in a particular situation and you have no right to do that. When Jesus said those words he was making a valid

2. Leroy Aden, "Pastoral Counseling as Christian Perspective," in Peter Homans, ed., *The Dialogue between Theology and Psychology* (Chicago: University of Chicago Press, 1968).

contradiction of the legalists in his day who always looked at behavior and almost nothing else. You remember—about praying in private and praying in public? It's too simplistic to take that statement by Jesus and say that the inner thought is *always* the same as an inner deed. Let me see . . . all right; if you do that with his statement, then you make a shambles of Jesus' temptations. To be consistent, you would have to say that when Jesus felt the temptations—and he would have had to feel them to make them real—then his feeling of temptation was the same as giving in to the temptation! Do you see what I'm saying?
Carter: Well—(long pause). Yes, I see your point. I guess I did get a little too excited and disturbed at myself. But I do have that feeling. And what does it mean?

The Development of Sexuality within the Tradition

That statement, "But I do have that feeling. And what does it mean?" now lays open the path for an examination of Carter's experience. To suggest that a counseling session of one hour—or even fifty hours—will lay Carter open like a book is erroneous. But there are "Carter-like signs" in every clergyman's sexual history and these become important examination points.

William J. Carter, now pastor of Union Church of Urbanville, was born thirty-seven years ago in a small town which served as the shopping center for the surrounding rural areas. His father started as a stock boy in a hardware store, worked up to clerk, and with the death of the owner joined two other clerks in buying the business. It was a good business but there was never an excess of money. Young Carter learned early to help at home and in the store. His mother was a housewife and reared two additional children, a sister three years younger and a brother five years younger than Bill. The family belonged to a local church and attendance was expected of the three children, particularly in Sunday school.

When William was eleven years old he participated with another boy in a rather typical sexual exploration session. The boys were seen by a neighbor who reported it to William's parents. William was paddled by his father and told to "never let me catch you doing anything like that again." As part of his punishment, William was given extra work to do at the hardware store. He did not fully understand what all was involved in what he had done and no explanation was given. It seemed to be taken for granted that he understood, and this was underscored by joking references from his peers who, it seemed, had all had experiences such as his in exploration, discovery, and punishment.

At the age of thirteen he had a nocturnal emission which was quite traumatic. He thought, when awakened by it, that he had "wet the bed" and was in terror of being treated as a child by his parents and punished. He did his best to conceal it, but after several such incidents, he realized one day that his mother noticed the evidence on his pajamas. He avoided his mother for the remainder of that day. That evening his father called him to his bedroom and in stern tones warned him against "playing with himself." Once again he was told to "never do anything like that again." William was in distress at this statement because he did not understand what his father meant and could not control the nocturnal emissions. By the age of fourteen, William had learned from his peers both the meaning of wet dreams and the practice of masturbation. He now carefully concealed all evidence of this from his parents.

In the fall of his fourteenth year, an evangelist came to their church for a week of services and William attended several of the meetings. He was as fascinated by what happened in the services as he was at what was preached. For one early evening, before the main service, the evangelist announced a meeting "for boys only." William's parents sent him.

It was at this meeting that William heard for the first time what was really wrong with nocturnal emissions, masturbation, and a new idea which the evangelist called "messing around with girls." He heard how nocturnal emissions were the result of impure and evil thoughts, masturbation was injurious to a young man's health, and dealings with girls (particularly the wrong kind) always led to heartaches for parents and tragedy for the boy. And, finally, he heard how God was opposed to such practices, had clearly stated this in the Bible, and would punish those who persisted in such practices. William stopped masturbating for one whole week. The nocturnal emissions continued and William hoped God would forgive him.

Except for such events as the senior high school dances, William dated infrequently. He spent most of his time working at the store. He left for college at age seventeen, planning to major in business administration and perhaps to join his father in the hardware business.

The state university proved to be a time of both liberation and constriction. Liberation occurred in his exposure to subject materials, heterogeneous peers, and varying life styles. Constriction occurred in developing a defensive posture by selecting out of the many influences those which were familiar and comfortable. Thus, he heard many stories of sexual enterprise and activity but for himself kept sex at the level of dormitory talk. He dated occasionally and sometimes was troubled with sexual feelings, but he did not date outside a circle of coeds whose general background paralleled his own. Masturbation continued to be his sexual expression but now sexual fantasies were added to it as a result of the stories which he heard.

Toward the end of his junior year, he expressed doubts about the business world and returning to his father's store. At the same time, a friendly relationship with a local minister in the university town started him thinking about studying for ministry. In the middle of his senior year he made his decision, met with a denominational committee which commended him for his sincerity, and applied to a theological seminary.

Bill's life at the theological seminary added two factors important to his later problem. First, the facades of prohibitive injunction, single celibacy, and social conformity were unwritten but assumed at the seminary and, when necessary, rigidly maintained. In fact, Bill found that attitudes toward sex were much the same as at the university, except that at the seminary it went underground. Whispers among small groups of friends, jokes, passing ribald remarks were steady signals of an intensity kept under the surface. Yet at no time did the administration or faculty see this aspect of student life as important to education. Sexuality was not considered part of a theological student's life.

The second factor was when Bill met Marge. She was two years younger than he, a secretary four years out of business school, and a member of the church to which he was assigned for field education. He was attracted to her and dated her with increasing frequency. For the first time Bill fell in love. With Marge he moved toward a new recognition of sexuality. What had formerly been a self-centered feeling was in process of transference to Marge. There was a strong desire for sexual expression with each other which they tried to meet by heavy petting. They were somewhat frustrated by this, however, and Bill felt guilty about it at times. As graduation and ordination approached, they were married.

Their sexual life in marriage was uneventful. Marge was less responsive than Bill had hoped for, but he made few demands because he didn't really expect much and he was engrossed in his work. By the time he was thirty-five they had two children and married life had become comfortably routine.

Only a viewpoint sensitive to sexual growth and attitudes allows the roots of Carter's crisis to become visible. Examination of his sexual life history, therefore, reveals at least four reasons why he encountered such difficulty in counseling with Betty Wilson.

First, sexuality in Carter's life always had a furtive quality about it. Except for the time when Carter was sent by his parents to hear the talk on sex by the evangelist, sex was kept in an underground status. None of the significant people in Carter's life dealt with the subject in open fashion, from his parents through his professors at the theological seminary. The subject of sex was discussed with peers, but always at a sub rosa level, and with the strong implication that it was not something to bring out into the open. His overt expressions of sexuality were either in the form of masturbation (significantly called the "secret vice" in some sexual literature) or in petting episodes in his premarital history which, in light of his background, were frustratingly guilt-

producing and not open for discussion even with Marge. A meas-
urement of the intensity of Carter's feelings in his encounter with
Betty Wilson is the fact that for the first time in his life, he went to a
counselor to discuss sex in an open fashion.

Second, judgments and attitudes toward sex are always in the
form of opposites (dichotomies). The use of dichotomy-style
thinking is seen in the positing of opposites in relation to sex:
good-bad; nice-not nice; clean-dirty; open-hidden. The use of such
a thought pattern about sex caused Carter to constantly place sex
at one extreme of his life and connect it to unfavorable attitudes.
Thus, as an adolescent, it was possible to divide girls into two
kinds: those who did (bad) and those who did not (good). His later
college life expanded this division to include both men and
women, but with the same adjectives: men and women who did
(bad) and those who did not (good).

Such a style of thinking allows no room for intermediate classifications between the extremes. What boys and girls did, clas-
sified as bad, allowed for no gradations except as peer discussion
might indicate what kinds of things they did (all bad). Therefore,
when Carter's usual non-thinking about sex (good) was inter-
rupted by his sexual thoughts about Betty Wilson (bad), the result
was to create severe dissonance for him by striking at his self-
image. For if he thought such thoughts (bad) and Betty Wilson
had not created the occasion for them (good), then he must be
bad.

Such thought about sex as "bad" makes it extremely difficult
for someone such as Carter to reorient himself to accepting the
affirmative aspects in the tradition concerning human sexuality.
While he undoubtedly could accept sex in marriage as good because of the love connected with it, there would still be a tinge of
doubt which would lead him to feel that sex in marriage is more to
be allowed than enjoyed.

Third, sexuality is dealt with in terms of law and codes. If
dichotomous thinking about sex occurs, then it follows that, since
sex is bad and is the general depository of negative adjectives, the
point of control is at the point of the exercise of sex. Any expres-

sion of sex by Carter as a boy is forbidden, and this injunction carried over even into such matters as nocturnal emissions. Not surprisingly, when he later feels sexual attraction to Betty Wilson, it comes forth in his mind as a breaking of a law or code rather than an expression of his sexuality which, not acted upon, carried little ethical burden.

Without any intermediate gradations in the scale between sex as bad and no sex as good, Carter has difficulty finding any difference in varied expressions of human sexuality. Any outbreak of sex in any form—thought or action—immediately carries an equal stigma. Thought repression, therefore, is as important to him as the repression of any desires which might lead to sexual activity. Throughout his developing life, Carter was exposed only to a limiting, restricting approach to sex which, since sex was bad, he saw as logical and proper.

Fourth, sexuality is a source of guilt. When as a boy Carter was exposed to sexual activity, it either brought punishment or, if not discovered, was viewed by him as an act deserving of punishment. The evangelist added the element of God's punishment on sexual activity, thus solidifying guilt as part of sex. What Carter's parents might not discover could not be hidden from God. Therefore sex unspoken and unacted was nevertheless equivalent to an act, and hence subject to punishment. The result of any sexual activity, with the exception of marital sex, was a feeling of guilt—that is, fit for punishment. Even within marriage, it would be most unlikely that Carter would be able to see sex as a pleasurable experience. More likely, he would see sexual relations in terms of marriage fulfillment, hence less punishable, and therefore less guilt.

Achieving New Perspective

Given these themes which pervade the history of Carter's sexual life, the final question is this: With all the rigidities and controls surrounding his expression of sexuality, how did his feelings manage to break through? To discover the answer to this question, we return to the dialogue:

Miller: Bill, I know your background pretty well . . . and you've had a struggle with some of the things that have bothered me too—things like sex as being bad and how God is against it and stuff like that. Yet I confess that with all those attitudes toward sex in my past, I still have some strong feelings sexually. Let me ask you again—is this really the first time you've had such a feeling since you were married?

Carter: Yes, Jim—that's the honest truth. I've never had a sexual feeling like this before that I can recall. I did at times when I was in college—I think I said this—but not since marriage.

Miller: OK—so we're different at that point. Now let me ask one more question. Was there anything that occurred recently that you can connect with this incident with Betty? You know—did you think of anything in connection with it . . . anything sexual . . . anything like that . . . or that happened?

Carter: No, I can't think of a thing . . . really. (long pause—Miller waits) Well, there was one thing, just the night before . . . but . . . yes, it might have something to do with it.

You may recall I told you last week I was going to the reception for Earl Myers who was recently elected pastor at First Church? Well, I went . . . and afterward, as I said goodby to Earl, he asked me to wait, saying he wanted to talk to me. So I waited and when the others had gone, he sat down and said, "Bill, I'm so mad I could walk out of this place." Naturally I was surprised and asked him what had happened.

He said, "Well, first of all, you know my wife, Arlene, is pregnant—about five months now, I guess. Anyway, I was walking around and some old biddy came up to me with a frown on her face and said, 'Pastor, how could you?' I didn't know what the hell she was talking about, so I just said, 'Could what? I don't know what you mean.' And then she nodded toward Arlene and said, 'She's pregnant. How could you?' And with that, she walked away. I was so stunned I couldn't think of anything to say. And the more I think about it the madder I get. Can you imagine that? I did something I shouldn't have done—and my wife's pregnant! How does that woman think we got our first child—by immaculate conception?"

Well, I talked to Earl a little while, calmed him down, and I left.

But, you know, that bothered me . . . and I kept thinking about it. What do church members think we are? . . . and I've about come to the conclusion that they think—and want us—to be non-sexed people. To not be a man . . . I don't know . . . but it made me mad, too. . . . (pause)

Hey, I wonder. . . .

Miller: Now, good . . . go on . . . finish it.

Carter: I never thought of that. Do you think that my response to Betty was . . . well, a kind of protest in its own way—a "hey, I'm a man" kind of statement? That's incredible, really. . . .

Miller: So you were asserting yourself as a man. . . .

Carter: Right. And I really wasn't making any sexual moves toward Betty. But I was feeling . . . kind of protesting . . . just letting it out because of my anger . . . and I suppose I felt so good in doing it that I wanted to see her again. But maybe not really to see her, maybe more, to continue the feeling I had.

Miller: This new feeling . . . it felt good. . . .

Carter: Yes, it did . . . (pause) I guess I've spent a lot of time trying to be above it all. (pause) You start from the time you're a kid. Sex is always wrong . . . and if you're really trying to be Christian, you pick up steadily a feeling against sex until everytime you acknowledge it, you feel guilty about it.

And, finally, you just push it away—except at times when it won't push away—and you begin to act as if it's no part of your life.

But, you know, it *is* a part of your life, if only . . . somehow . . . we could learn from the beginning how to handle it. But it sure gets twisted.

Miller: So that growing out of this, as . . . negativism and repression that goes on . . . uh . . . the role of the minister gets mixed up with it . . . .

Carter: Right . . . and people seem to expect it. Imagine: "Pastor, how could you?"

The Pastor as Asexual

Carter's protest against expecting the clergyman to be asexual is significant, for the roots of such an expectation are deep. Nor is this attitude about clergymen always as apparent as in this dialogue.

The source of the asexual attitude is found in a cultural view which is undergirded by a negative view of sex. This cultural view, based upon untenable biological presuppositions, sees certain traits as inherently masculine and others as inherently feminine. Thus, aggressiveness, assertiveness, and nonemotionality are viewed as masculine traits, while passivity, warmth, and gentleness are seen as feminine traits. Upon such personality traits is built a sex role classification in society, and from such classification definitions of sexuality are derived. Research indicates that such traits are learned, not inherent, and sex role classifications are coming under scrutiny; but the structure and residual cultural imprinting of this system is still present and must be recognized.[3] The ministry as a profession has suffered extensively from these sex role classifications because the exercise of a pastoral ministry—caring for and serving people—requires a predominate use of what culture calls "feminine" traits. To be sure, these "feminine" traits are utilized in all people-oriented professions such as medicine and the clinical practice of psychology. But in these professions the person of the practitioner is more easily separated from the practice, and clientele expectations are not imposed in as direct a fashion. So the ministry as a profession has tended to attract some persons who are satisfied to express only these traits and, in so doing, deny their total sexuality.

In actuality, the full expression of ministry includes both masculine and feminine trait expressions. For example, the minister as prophet is expressive of the masculine role. The uneasiness of congregations in the face of the prophetic role indicates the kind of difficulties the pastor faces when he leaves a less intensive expression of his work.[4] Only recently has pastoral counseling, moving away from structured passivity, joined other practitioners of counseling in a balanced trait expression: "Effective treatment procedures involve both the traditionally feminine dimensions such as sensitivity and warmth as well as the more masculine dimensions such as genuineness and confrontation. . . ."[5]

The pastor who strongly emphasizes pastoral concerns tends to operate in feminine trait styles and, lacking masculine expression in his work, assumes an asexual status in the eyes of the

3. J. Money, J. G. Hampson, and J. L. Hampson, "Imprinting and the Establishment of Gender Role," *Archives of Neurology and Psychiatry* (1957), 77:333–36.
4. C. Y. Glock, B. B. Ringer, and E. R. Babbie, *To Comfort and to Challenge* (Berkeley: University of California Press, 1967), pp. 119–25.
5. Robert R. Carkhuff, *Helping and Human Relations,* vol. 2 (New York: Holt, Rinehart and Winston, 1969), p. 284. See also Robert E. Elliott, "Motherly and Fatherly Modes of Pastoral Care" in William B. Oglesby, Jr., ed., *The New Shape of Pastoral Theology* (Nashville: Abingdon Press, 1969).

congregation—and, all too often, in his own eyes too. He becomes a victim of the unfortunate definition of a minister as one
who sits in the grandstand with the women explaining the game of
life being played by the men on the field below. Traditionally, one
who may sit with the women while the men are away is neither
masculine nor feminine, but a eunuch.

The pastor, however, who has come to grips with his own
sexuality and neither denies it nor needs to force its expression,
can live comfortably with whatever traits are necessary for his
work. He no longer feels the need to prove his masculinity nor to
deny his caring concern for others. In his work he can be God's
man, himself at all times. And in doing this, he refutes the sex
role classifications by which society limits and controls the expression of the total being.

Guilt and Growth

Over a third cup of coffee, Carter and Miller continue to ex-
plore the problem of a pastor's own sexuality and people's attitudes toward it.

Miller: It is a problem, and it does make you angry. But where are we in
it—where do we go from here?
Carter: Well, I suppose we just go on being men, whatever that means to
us. But, you know, it seems to me that you can't really be a man—or
be a sexual person—as long as you do keep it covered over and held
down and. . . .
Miller: By keeping a lid on it . . . and I've been as bad as you were in this
one. I left out some of my feelings at times and it made me as disturbed
and . . . guilty . . . as you said you felt.
Carter: But the point is, I guess, that recognizing your own sexuality
doesn't mean you're going to suddenly start running around and chas-
ing women . . . in fact, it means just the opposite. You don't have to
prove anything.
  Now the goal is to be the best of what you are . . . uh . . . as a man
and a person. And that means you get in control of your own life . . .
which makes it kind of scary, what with the rules dropping out . . .
but. . . .
Miller: Yeah . . . but there is some kind of a check on it all, even when
the rigidities disappear. How that works, I'm not sure. But at least,

we're free to be ourselves. And that feels good—and maybe that's
what you felt, more than just a sexual feeling toward Betty . . . just a
feeling of being yourself.
Carter: Could be . . . but I'll tell you one thing . . . I bet I'll be a better
counselor for having gone through this. At least I can start to understand the whole business of sex better than before . . . which reminds
me: What about Marge? I want to talk this over with her.

Pastors Carter and Miller continued their discussion for some
time (edited here from the tapes of four sessions). Carter decided
to keep his appointment with Betty, feeling that he understood
the dynamics of the situation well enough now to make it helpful
for her.

It is interesting to note that as the session moved along, the
distinctive lines between counselor and counselee disappeared.
Both men were groping for answers from their own experience
and newly-discovered insight. Much more understanding and insight would be needed before major resolutions of their problems
could occur, and Miller needed this as much as Carter.

Both men would need to come to grips with the problem of
guilt. Carter had expressed his feeling well: "But I did think
it—and I still feel it . . . I feel guilty as hell." Miller, much later in
the discussion, agreed: "I left out some of my feelings at times
and it made me as disturbed and . . . guilty . . . as you said you
felt." In both men, the expression of sexual feelings had created a
feeling of guilt. But insight into the reasons lying behind such
expression would not of itself eliminate the guilt feelings, for guilt
is a dynamic which accompanies and instructs the shifting viewpoint on sexuality. It is, in fact, a dynamic which is threaded
through all the developmental stages of internal controls and conscience.

The child, in learning a moral code, internalizes that code given
to him by parents and society, although always having it subject
to his sometimes limited understanding of it. In essence, however, it is not *his* code but one which he receives from outside
himself. This code is reinforced by both approval and punishment, usually by parents, and the child acts within the code to

receive approval and to avoid punishment. As the child develops into adolescence, and ultimately adulthood, the code is either transplanted in toto to the adult, or it is modified and even discarded at times through more experience and new learnings. Crucial to understanding this process is the recognition that guilt is the accompanying dynamic both in the maintenance of a code and in changing of codes from an inherited one to a reconstructed one. Guilt comes with the word "ought," and this word applies the harsh realities of approval or punishment without regard to the stage of development.

Carter's case is typical of the many in contemporary society in which the moral code on sex is translated from childhood to adulthood without major revision. The "ought" which was applied originally by his parents and society is basically the same one he has carried into adulthood. This easy carryover through successive growth periods without essential modification occurs because of the hidden and furtive aspects of sex which, never recognized in open fashion, are controlled by an unusually heavy restriction. Carter, in his own life style, was an observer of the sexual scene but never a participant in it except as physiological feelings took him into masturbation and, later, heavy petting. Even his marriage excused him from recognizing and dealing with his own sexuality because he legitimized the sexual expression by linking it to love and keeping the two inseparable. Important as love is to sex, it served in Carter's case to hinder his understanding of himself.

When in confronting his own sexuality with the visit of Betty Wilson he had to face the subject, Carter's immediate reaction was disturbance and the feeling of guilt which caused a reinforcement of his childhood code. But beyond this reinforcement, there was also a different feeling of guilt as Carter looked at sexuality in a new way during the incident with Pastor Myers and during his counseling session with Pastor Miller. So there was guilt reinforcing the old code and guilt as he acknowledged the new view; but the two forms of guilt are quite different.

The first form of guilt, that reinforcing the old, had fear as its fundamental base, for transgression of the old code carried punishment-reinforcement with it. The "ought" was essentially an "ought not": you ought not to disobey, and if you do you will be punished. The demand of this guilt was negative, and when seen as inherited by the person rather than developed within the person, it is recognizable as what Freud called neurotic guilt. Springing from the fear of change, of moving ahead, it is a guilt that works against the development of new vision or new understanding, without regard for the benefit to the person. This guilt rises from the past to haunt Carter: You will be punished if you change. But who will punish? Even more difficult for Carter is the fact that the old code was reinforced by the visiting evangelist in his boyhood, so that God becomes the one who punishes, not just the memory of past parental correction. So Carter, looking at the new, feels himself ready to become the victim of God's displeasure: "But I *did* think it—and I still feel it, God help me. . . ."

The impact of the recognition of his own sexuality plus the experience of Pastor Myers moved Carter, with Miller's help, to a consideration of a new position on sexuality. With this movement, a new form of guilt arises. It is a type of guilt which has a base in the anxiety created by change and choice. But it is also a guilt produced by past decisions omitted and an anxiety-guilt about decisions in the future. However, this anxiety now produced a guilt of growth. Thus McKenzie says:

> It is the passing from the "borrowed morality" of the Super-ego to the free morality of conscience where *oughts, commands* and prohibitions have become moral guides and not moral policemen. . . . Thus we pass from the negative conscience which functions autonomously and lies over against our personality and indeed is at war with it, to one integrated with our personality.[6]

The new guilt now accompanies a positive approach toward a new position on sexuality with a potential for both growth and errors on the way to that growth.

6. John G. McKenzie, *Guilt: Its Meaning and Significance* (Nashville: Abingdon Press, 1962), pp. 48–49.

It is important for the pastoral counselor to be aware of this shifting aspect of guilt and the forms it takes in the area of human sexuality. When the old restrictive codes of sexuality begin to break, the alternative is not a libertarian or completely secular position on sex, as the concerned individual might think. Rather, the change in attitude and the adoption of an affirmative viewpoint about sexuality also has its roots within a biblical-theological tradition which emphasizes the goodness of creation and the expansive possibilities of human life.[7] This new rootage in an affirmative tradition frees men, not to excess, but to a new position of responsibility and concern for others. The guilt which accompanies the new position is the guardian of it. Free from restrictive law, it is a self-actualizing guilt which the pastoral counselor needs to recognize, preserve, and help the individual to refine.

The possibilities for a mature approach to human sexuality are now available to both Carter and Miller. But these possibilities are open because they are based on biblical-theological affirmations about human sexuality rather than on negative attitudes which bound them to the past.

7. Such an emphasis creates its own necessary limitations. Robert W. Jenson writes: "The biblical proclamation of creation . . . puts man under God, so that what man needs or wants . . . is not necessarily the last word. If there is the Creator, we are not *above* the creation, we are *in* it . . . man has his role *within* the story of creation; he is not its author. *Story and Promise* (Philadelphia: Fortress Press, 1973), pp. 149–50.

4. Counseling Women in Their Changing Role

"She's her father's daughter!" remarked Mrs. Ames as she placed the phone back on the receiver. "She's as independent as they come. I pity the man *she* marries . . . that is, *if* she marries."

Pastor Ames was amused but pleased by his wife's comments about their daughter. It was true. Judy, now a third year law student, had a mind of her own. She certainly seemed to know what she wanted out of life, and she worked hard to achieve her goals. "Actually," Bob Ames thought, "she's quite a person! Who would have thought twenty-five years ago that my daughter would be studying in one of the nation's top law schools? A son, but not a daughter."

A woman lawyer—when Pastor Ames was in school that was a rarity, a subject of ridicule. Indeed, the issues of women's equal rights, sex role socialization, and consciousness raising would have seemed strange and humorous to most of his classmates. In those days women wanted to be wives and mothers. Oh, they worked before marriage, and even after if the family was in financial crisis, but by and large they were content to leave the professions to men. In some respects life was simpler then. At least a man could deal with women without worrying about whether he was being chauvinistic.

"I wonder how far I'd be in my thinking, if it weren't for Judy and her friends," he mused. It had been a shock to Bob Ames to realize just how constrictive the traditional ways of thinking about men and women were, and to discover how deeply ingrained these views were in his own attitudes. Through his daughter and her friends, he'd come to appreciate the desire of women to be treated as *persons,* not wives, not mothers, not sex objects.

53

Paternal prejudice aside, Bob did respect his daughter as a competent, capable person. He found Judy's vitality and ambition exciting. If only he could find a way to release that same vigor and confidence in the lives of some of the women with whom he was counseling.

Ten years ago, he had called it "the housewife's syndrome" when women came to him with vague complaints about depression, irritability, and fatigue. Romance had gone out of marriage and life seemed an endless round of serving meals, cleaning up, doing the laundry, and taxiing kids. Evenings found their husbands tired, inert, and conversationless before the television set. In those days, in good pastoral fashion, he had counseled such women toward better adjustment to their roles as wives and mothers. He stressed the importance of good nurture for children, emotional support for husbands, and encouraged them to get out of the house once in awhile. Now he listened with a different mentality and new understanding of the psychological fatigue and frustration women experienced in fitting themselves to their traditional roles.

The Frustrations of Wife and Mother

Mrs. Brown had phoned one afternoon and asked to see him. "Alan and I are in the middle of our first major disagreement. I need to talk this over with someone."

The disagreement turned out to be over Carol Brown's desire to get back into social work, a desire which her husband vigorously opposed.

"Alan is concerned about the children and insists that I ought to be at home with them. Of course, I'm concerned about the children. But, really, I think they wouldn't suffer from having a sitter come in five or six hours a day. In fact, it might even be better than having a frustrated mother to cope with. Pastor, I love my children, but I'm slowly going out of my mind. Life with two small children leaves me so little time for anything else. I think if I got back into the work I love, even part-time, I'd be a better mother.

"But Alan disagrees. He thinks it's my Christian duty to be at home. Am I being selfish and unfair to Alan?"

Pastor Ames had seen Carol on Monday. Tuesday, he heard a different version of the same inquiry: How can I be at once a Christian wife, mother, and person? This time it was Linda Chambers putting the question. She had contacted Pastor Ames at the suggestion of her husband, Tom.

"I don't know what's the matter with me. I feel like I'm coming apart. . . . Yet here I am, married to a fine Christian man. I have three healthy children . . . but I can't seem to get hold of myself. I must have spent the better part of this week crying. Of course, Tom doesn't appreciate my tears very much. I guess a lot of things are just getting me down.

"Tom is a good husband, but I don't think he realizes . . . well, I'm just not his *mother*. She's full of energy and very efficient. And he expects me to be the same. He wants meals on time, the house spotless, and me looking beautiful . . . with three active children that's no small feat. It seems I'm always behind. . . . But the thing that is really bothering me is . . . well . . . Tom wants another baby. He'd love to have a son. . . . I know how important that is to a man, but I just don't feel up to it. I *really don't!* But I feel awful about my own feelings. After all, he is head of the house. As a Christian I can't very well say no to my husband, can I?"

Both Carol and Linda, being Christian, were struggling with a traditional feminine model which understands fulfillment for the woman exclusively in the role of wife and mother. They were finding that the subordinate, serving nature of that role permits only minimal expression of a woman's individual uniqueness and potentiality.

Carol Brown had a master's degree in social work. She had held a responsible job for three years prior to the birth of her first child. Guided by the feminine model, she expected that when she quit her job she would find satisfaction in the role of wife and mother. That expectation was not met. For, although she loved her husband and children, she felt cut off from a part of herself.

Yet she was unsure of that feeling in terms of her understanding of Christian responsibility, and that uncertainty is what brought her to the pastor.

Linda Chambers had married Tom, five years her senior, shortly after her graduation from high school. She knew marriage was expected of her and was pleased at how her family had approved of Tom. Their pattern of married life followed a conservative Christian model: Tom was the head of his wife as Christ was head of the church and Linda was duly respectful. Yet Linda, after six years of marriage, was uneasy about achieving Tom's standards. Feeling unable to oppose her husband on the matter of another child, she found herself unhappy with her feelings of opposition. Sensing some lack of Christian spirit, she came to the pastor.

In a sense, each woman posed the same question to Pastor Ames: What insight does the Christian faith bring to bear on my role as a woman and my feelings as a person—how can I, with integrity, understand myself as wife, mother, Christian, and person?

Role Problems and Human Sexuality

At first impression, this question seems to have little to do with human sexuality. In fact, students in our seminary course on human sexuality are frequently surprised when we introduce material on sex roles and on the attitudes of men and women toward themselves and toward each other. The students argue, "What does socialization have to do with sex?" The fact is that in its effects sexuality goes beyond merely explicit sexual behavior to include the total expression of masculinity and femininity. It touches the concept of self and the social roles learned as appropriate for each sex. The way a woman thinks about herself as a woman lies behind *all* that she says and does, including sexual expression. Thus, the woman who views herself an inferior and understands her role as servile, brings these attitudes to the sexual relationship. In the same way, a man's sexual approach to a woman reflects his general attitudes about masculinity and femininity.

Problems related to how men and women view themselves and their roles are an important aspect of human sexuality, and they come to the pastoral counselor in varying forms. Typically they surface when sex role expectations are disappointed or when traditional sex models become constrictive under the pressures of contemporary change.

The experiences of Carol Brown and Linda Chambers can be viewed as typical of the present confusion over sex roles. Each woman, in her own situation, found the traditional model a problem, and each looked to the pastor for help in getting a Christian perspective on her desire to be more than the role specifications allowed.

The Tradition and Change

In responding to women like Carol Brown and Linda Chambers, the pastoral counselor has to take account of his tradition, which tends to view women from within the framework of a patriarchal society. In the biblical culture, women were chattels, the property of men, having no political rights and few social and legal ones. Consistent with the wider cultural milieu, they found their place on the fringe of a male-centered world.

The structure of modern society is drastically different. The change has been particularly rapid in recent times. The end of World War I marked a beginning decline of patriarchy, although its psychological hangover remains with us. Women have gained the right to vote and the right to higher education, and major social changes have begun to affect the role of wife and mother. Today, more women are working outside the home than ever before; 40 percent of the U.S. labor market is comprised of women. Medical science and technology have given the woman increasing control over her body, so that she can choose when or if she wants to have a child. Life expectancies have increased, with the result that the average woman can look forward to 25-30 years of living after her last child has left home. Concern with overpopulation has led to a de-emphasis on large families. In the light of contemporary life styles, it is no longer realistic to view women on the fringe of the social order, and no longer adequate to see the woman's role solely as that of wife and mother. Yet the view of woman as an inferior subordinate, whose chief occupation in life is to bear children and serve her family, still exerts strong influence as a Christian model. Biblical passages have been used to bolster and perpetuate that influence: Proverbs 31 describes the good wife who toils diligently in the service of her husband; certain passages from Paul's writings have been the mainstay for Christianizing the subordination of women:

> As in all congregations of God's people, women should not address the meeting. They have no licence to speak, but should keep their place as the law directs. If there is something they want to know, they can ask their own husbands at home. It is a shocking thing that a woman should address the congregation.   (1 Cor. 14:34–35)

> But I wish you to understand that, while every man has Christ for his Head, woman's head is man, as Christ's Head is God . . . . A man has no need to cover his head, because man is the image of God, and the mirror of his glory, whereas woman reflects the glory of man. For man did not originally spring from woman, but woman was made out of man; and man was not created for woman's sake, but woman for the sake of man; and therefore it is woman's duty to have a sign of authority on her head, out of regard for the angels.
> (1 Cor. 11:3–10)

Theologians as recent even as Karl Barth interpret Ephesians 5:21–24 as the pattern for marriage:

> Let him [man] stand to the woman in the same relation as Christ to His community by being to her the head in this sense, by being genuinely strong and kind in relation to her. If the woman understands the man's precedence and superiority in this sense, in the light of his task and function she will surely be willing not merely to accept but freely to embrace the subordination which befits her.[1]

1. Karl Barth, *On Marriage* (Philadelphia: Fortress Press, 1968), p. 14.

The influence of Paul's model on Linda Chambers was evident as she and Pastor Ames discussed her feelings about another pregnancy.

Pastor: How do you think Tom would react if you simply told him you weren't ready for another child?

Linda: I *couldn't* say that to him. It's all so confused. Even though I feel like I couldn't cope with another child . . . I *should* be able to. As Tom says, I'm not getting any younger. I know his mother had five children. It's like . . . well, if I were really Christian I'd want to give Tom another child. I've never really felt guilt like this before. I usually go along with Tom. This time, I just can't. I've prayed about it . . . I've worried about it, but . . . .

Pastor: It strikes me that you are asking an awful lot of a mother with three kids under the age of five. Why do you think you *should* be able to cope with the added responsibility of another child.

Linda: I guess because Tom expects it of me. After all, I *am* his wife. But somehow, lately . . . not a very good one.

As a Christian, Linda understood her involvement in marriage to mean that her role as wife and mother took precedence over her personal feelings and needs. The character of the role was derived mainly from what she perceived to be her husband's expectations. Tom's expressed desire for a son, however, trapped her between anxiety if she consented and guilt if she refused. Either way, the Christian model, as she understood it, led her to value herself in terms of her ability to carry out the role expected of her.

The Promise of Early Christianity

Paradoxically, Christianity in the beginning gave promise of becoming a liberating force for women. It turned upside down the old order and preached a new order of life based on relationships of *agape*. It rejoiced in the gifts of the spirit operative in women as well as in men. Paul caught this vision of a new order which erased all social barriers in Christ: "There is no such thing as Jew and Greek, slave and freeman, male and female; for you are all one person in Christ Jesus" (Gal. 3:28). Jesus' ministry made no distinctions between men and women as children of God and recipients of grace. His ministry was to persons. In fact, women appeared at the center of his activity: among his friends and followers, at the cross and tomb, and even as witnesses of his first resurrection appearance. As Conrad Bergendoff points out:

> One finds nowhere that Jesus ranks men and women. He treats each as an individual per se. The only pre-eminence he allows is that of service, "whosoever would be first among you shall be your servant." (Matt. 20:27) By the regard he shows to women, by the treatment he gives them in word and act, by the purity and universality of his love and ministry, Jesus Christ erased all lines of superiority or inferiority between men and women and placed all on the same level of grace.[2]

To examine the reasons why the vision of equality in Christ was lost in subsequent centuries would be interesting, but outside the scope of the present chapter.[3] The point is that, although that vision received spiritual interpretation, it never became social reality. Instead, sometime between the second and fourth centuries, Christianity became an institution in which women were again found in their subordinate place on the fringe of church life, with roles determined for them on the basis of sex differences.

In the twentieth century, if Christianity is to become a liberating force for persons, its attitudes on women need to be examined. The tradition needs reinterpretation and translation for contemporary life. The baseline for translation has its roots in Jesus' affirmation of men and women as persons, and in the gospel which calls persons to freedom and growth in Christ. Such a translation by the pastoral counselor has the potential for freeing

2. Margaret Sittler Ermarth, *Adam's Fractured Rib* (Philadelphia: Fortress Press, 1970), p. 17.
3. Rosemary Radford Ruether suggests in her article "Women's Liberation in Perspective," that antifemale prejudice was tightly interwoven with Greek dualism's prejudice against the body and its elevation of the spirit. Both prejudices entered the Christian tradition early in its development under the strong influence of dualism. The article appears in *Women's Liberation and the Church*, ed. Sarah Bentley Doely (New York: Association Press, 1970), pp. 26–36.

women to be persons, with all that such freedom might mean in contemporary life.

As Pastor Ames attempts translation of a contemporary Christian perspective toward women in his counseling with Carol Brown and Linda Chambers, he is aware of their common question: How much self-expression does my role as wife and mother allow? But as always in counseling, the unique experience of each counselee requires a different and uniquely individual approach.

Mother as Person

Carol Brown, 31, was born the youngest of three girls in an achievement-oriented family. Her father was a successful design engineer. Although her own mother did not "work," she was deeply involved in church and community affairs. All three daughters were encouraged to attend college. Carol and her oldest sister went on to graduate school. After receiving her master's degree in social work, Carol became affiliated with a small private psychiatric center. It was while she was working there that she met Alan and fell in love. They married and she continued work until three months before the birth of their first child. Carol had no doubts about her new role as wife and mother; she expected to find in it complete fulfillment as a woman. Within three years, however, she realized that being a wife and mother was not enough. She needed the fresh stimulation of meaningful work outside her home. When she told her husband that she wanted to go back to her old job, a solution that seemed appropriate to her, she met resistance. The reasons for Alan's resistance came out in their first joint counseling session with Pastor Ames.

Pastor: Alan, I've already talked with Carol, so perhaps we could begin by having you state your point of view.
Alan: I just don't see why Carol is so set on getting a job. I know taking care of the kids isn't always easy, but most women seem to enjoy being at home with their children . . . I really don't understand Carol at this point.
Pastor: Carol? Can you help Alan here?
Carol: I've tried to explain before that I make a lousy full-time mother. I'm irritable and short with the children. I just feel frustrated. I miss the adult interaction I had on the job and I miss doing some of the

things I know I do well. I think part-time work would be the answer. I
know other women who have gone to work and made good babysitting
arrangements for their children.

Alan: But, Carol, couldn't this wait until the children are older? I
thought that's what we had kind of agreed on when you stopped working. Kids need their own mother. A sitter is just *not* the same . . . .
Look, if it's money . . . I told you, I'll look for a second job.

Carol: No, it's not money. Maybe it's just me—maybe I'm not a normal
mother. . . . When we talked three years ago, I really thought I'd
enjoy being a full-time mother. I never expected I'd feel this way. . . .
Somehow I know I'd be better with the children if I were happier.

Alan: I had no idea you were so unhappy!

Carol: Maybe that's a poor word—frustrated would describe my feelings
better.

Alan: Well, it seems to me that—here's where Christianity comes in,
doesn't it, Pastor? A Christian mother should be willing to sacrifice a
bit and stay with her children while they need her!

Alan's appeal to Christianity for support of his position required a response. Pastor Ames began to lay out for examination
some of the hidden assumptions in the Browns' conversation.

First assumption: Alan believed that a Christian model for
motherhood dictated against Carol's return to work. What Alan
identified as Christian is, in fact, the cultural belief that "a
woman's place is in the home." This proscription derives from a
day when sex roles were clearly defined—the man provided for
and protected the family unit and the woman bore children,
reared them, and managed the home. That clarity and distinctiveness between men's work and women's work is blurred in
today's complex, technological world. The roles and jobs necessary for the operation of modern society are highly diversified and
continue to multiply in number. Many of these jobs are carried
out by both men and women. As someone noted, the pushbutton
doesn't care whether the pressing finger is masculine or feminine.
With increasing educational and job opportunities, many women
receive training in a vocation other than motherhood. Carol was,
in fact, trained professionally just as Alan was. There is nothing

specifically Christian that speaks *against* Carol's working outside the home. It could even be argued that the Christian emphasis on personal growth and social responsibility speaks for the best use of her training and abilities; this consideration could indicate a return to work for Carol.

Second assumption: Alan and Carol together believed that a "normal" woman finds completeness in motherhood. Here, both have felt the influence of a socialization process which considered marriage and motherhood as ultimate goals for girls. The myth underlying traditional socialization is that women are not truly fulfilled until they marry and bear children. Whereas little boys are asked, "What do you want to be when you grow up?" little girls, it is assumed, will want to be wives and mothers. Parents carefully select appropriate toys for girls (dolls) and guide their daughters into play activities (house) which reinforce the expectation that marriage will provide the basic structure and meaning for their lives. Many school systems have undergirded this socialization process by routing girls into home economics courses designed to teach the needed skills for homemaking and child care.

So Alan, baffled by Carol's discontent, and Carol, wondering whether she is a normal woman, need to examine critically the myth underlying the traditional socialization which has influenced their lives. This myth is vulnerable on two counts: (1) It stereotypes women instead of viewing them as individuals; (2) It assumes that because women are biologically equipped to carry, deliver, and nurse children, mothers are also the best equipped psychologically and emotionally to love and nurture their children.

The first point is self-explanatory. The assumption in the second runs counter to clinical evidence since Freud indicating that the relationship of mother to child has the potential of unfortunate possibilities for the child. Mothering, in fact, can be a "nurturing" of neurosis in childhood. Thus, instead of viewing Carol's frustration with full-time mothering as deviation from a mythic norm, it will be more constructive for Alan and Carol to consider the effects of her continued frustration upon the network of family relationships.

Third assumption: Alan believed that Carol's constant presence is not only necessary for good mothering, but is irreplaceable; quantity of time is more important than quality of time. Research from the behavioral sciences, indicates, however, that total family dynamics are more important in influencing personality formation than is the mother's constant presence. Although children do need constant care and loving attention, such nurture can be provided by people other than the biological mother.

Moreover, the quality of mothering often suffers when child care is viewed as the work of the mother. Such a view runs the risk of minimizing the importance of fathering and of placing the emphasis on a mother's *doing* rather than the child's *being*. The insight of Sidney Cornelia Callahan is an important one:

> You don't mold a person or work on him as you do on a project or impersonal task. Child rearing is a human relationship, a mutual sharing of human potential, which is best done in some bigger context. Adults are too aggressive and high powered to center totally on a child's upbringing, which is slow and depends more on the activity of the child rather than the adult. I, for one, am a much better mother when my work is absorbing lots of energy and I am able to live with my children rather than work on them.[4]

Fourth assumption: Alan believed that "a Christian mother should be willing to sacrifice a bit and stay with her children while they need her—here's where Christianity comes in, doesn't it, Pastor?"

In response to Alan's question, Pastor Ames suggested a homework assignment to be carried out over the coming weekend. To help Alan understand that nature of the sacrifice

4. Sidney Cornelia Callahan, "A Christian Perspective on Feminism," *Women's Liberation and the Church*, p. 44.

under discussion, Alan and Carol were to act out a role reversal for two days. Beginning Saturday morning, Alan was to assume Carol's role and take charge of three-and-one-half-year-old David and two-year-old Christy. Carol was to leave the house each day at 8:30 A.M. and not return until 6:00 P.M. After a few mild objections, both Carol and Alan agreed to carry out the assignment.

Reactions to the strange weekend were discussed at the following counseling session.

Alan: I have mixed feelings. In some ways it was fun proving to myself that I could do it. But it was difficult too. You really don't get much done with those two live wires around.

Carol: I had mixed reactions too. Having two whole days to myself was a luxury. But I was anxious about Alan. He's never taken care of the children like that before.

Pastor: I asked you to do this primarily so that you, Alan, could get a feel for what Carol's daily life is like . . . so you would have a better understanding of what you're asking of her.

Alan: I've been thinking about that. And I know two days is a lot different from everyday. But I still don't think it's all that frustrating.

Pastor: OK. I'm going to ask you something that may strike you as ridiculous at first . . . How do you think it would work if Carol got a job and you left your work to be at home with the children?

Alan was confounded. Then the thoughts began to pour out. It was absurd. It wouldn't work. He couldn't leave the firm. The kids need their mother. They'd be confused. What about money? Carol wouldn't make as much as he made. What would the neighbors say?

Each of these reactions formed the basis for discussion over the next few counseling sessions. Gradually, Alan began to see that he was himself unwilling to make the kind of sacrifice he was asking Carol to make. With consistent effort by Pastor Ames to keep Carol, the person, the focal point in the issue, Alan began to understand her motivation for returning to social work. While it was difficult for him to keep from interpreting this desire on her part as a rejection of her mother role, he finally conceded that

Carol's moods and frame of mind did have an effect on the children. And after considerable effort by Carol to find good substitute child care, Alan agreed that part-time work for Carol was a viable option.

What began, then, as a question of Christian perspective for Carol, who desired to be more than a mother, developed into a question of consciousness-raising for Alan. He had been viewing the problem with a form of tunnel vision: He was able to see only one aspect of the total picture, and even that was filtered through the traditional model he held of the mother's role.

At the cognitive level, Pastor Ames worked to expand Alan's vision of the problem by introducing important related factors: changing life styles, new views toward women, thinking from the behavioral sciences on sex role socialization, and general human development. He used role reversal to deal with the problem at emotional and behavioral levels. His goal was to help Alan widen his tunnel vision of Carol, the mother, and to see also Carol, the person, who was mother in much the same way that Alan, the person, was father. With understanding and support from Pastor Ames, Carol too was able to view herself as a person, a responsible mother and a Christian, with these varying roles enhancing rather than inhibiting one another.

Persons in Relationship

Counseling with Alan and Carol Brown called for Pastor Ames to aid them in resolving the role conflict they both perceived between mother, Christian, and person. Linda Chambers's presenting problem was articulated, not as a role conflict, but as a personal struggle to live up to the model held of a Christian wife. The model required her to subordinate personal desires to her responsibilities as wife and mother and to merge her feelings with those of her husband. Where these feelings did not mesh, Linda tended to evaluate herself negatively.

Linda: So, what it all comes down to, I guess, is that I'm not a very good wife . . . and not much of a Christian.

Pastor: How do you think Tom feels? Does he indicate that you're not a good wife?

Linda: Oh, I don't know. . . . He never actually said that. . . . But he does get impatient with me.

Pastor: I think it would help a lot if you knew where Tom *does* stand —what his feelings really are . . . whether he really does want another child as much as you believe he does. . . . How would it be if I stopped over at the house some evening this week and the three of us talked this out? How about Wednesday evening? He knows you're seeing me?

Linda: Yes. Wednesday would be fine. But I'm still a little anxious about it all.

Pastor: Well, let's sit down and talk, the three of us, and then we'll decide where we go from there. And by the way . . . your remark about not being much of a Christian . . . I guess we all feel that way at times. So hang in there.

On Wednesday evening, with the pastor's help, Linda began to share her feelings about having another child, and to talk openly about her difficulty in discussing her feelings with Tom. Her husband looked relieved.

Tom: Is that all it was? I knew something was the matter, with you crying all week. That's why I wanted you to talk with Pastor Ames. I didn't know what was wrong. . . . But why didn't you just say something?

Linda: I thought you'd be disappointed and maybe even angry. You know how much you've talked about a son.

Tom: Well, sure, I'd like to have a son. But even if we had another baby, there's no guarantee it'd be a boy. I was just talking. Gee, I know you're swamped. I wasn't going to push it. Why would I get angry about that?

Linda: Well, you *do* get angry at me . . . when the house is a mess or when the kids act up.

Tom: Sure, I get annoyed . . . and that usually gets some action. But that's different. I know another baby would be too much for you now. As I said, I was just talking.

Pastor: Well, there's no disagreement then as you say these things to one another. But why was it so tough for Linda to talk about? Why didn't Tom make it clear that he was kind of pipe dreaming about a son? And what would have happened between you had Tom been set on having another child now? It strikes me that the pattern of relationship you have . . . almost sets up misunderstandings. Between your doubt in your own feelings, Linda, and your mixed signals, Tom, communications get confused . . . and somehow you miss saying some pretty important things to one another. I'd like to talk more with you both about some of these things.

The three agreed to meet again, but for a new purpose: to look more closely at the dynamics of Linda and Tom's relationship. Pastor Ames briefly indicated several areas of concern: First, there was Paul's biblical analogy to be examined; while the analogy itself pointed to mutual love and commitment in the husband-wife relationship, the Chamberses tended to fasten on the ancient sociological structure in which the analogy was cast, thus limiting full expression of mutuality in their relationship. Second, Linda and Tom each brought to marriage certain expectations about sex role which needed to be reviewed and weighed. Third, important to the marital relationship was the development of better communication.

Tom and Linda were thoughtful as they began to react to Pastor Ames' remarks:

Tom: I'm beginning to see that our marriage is pretty much a one-way operation. I call the shots and Linda follows. I just never thought of it quite that way.

Linda: I guess I'm partly responsible for that, Tom. But I wish we *could* share more . . . be closer.

Tom: Whew! I'm not sure how to tackle that one . . . or even what it means, in terms of changing things. But if it will help Linda . . . help us . . . I'm willing to try.

The Chamberses met weekly with Pastor Ames for six months, individually and jointly. Although they both had motivation to improve their marriage, the effort involved in growing and changing was not easy. A pattern of relationship had been well established through six years of living together and through prior learning. Both were, in a sense, products of a socialization process which stereotyped men as dominant, aggressive, nonemotional, and masters of their environment, and women as passive, yielding, emotional, and accommodating. Tom had learned to be his own man, to make his wishes known, to get what he wanted, but he felt acutely uncomfortable with expressions of emotion, excepting anger. Linda learned to be feminine: to be soft, to be yielding, and to please, but she had difficulty in self-assertion because it carried the risk of disapproval. Each brought to the marriage a need structure built upon these models of masculinity and femininity. Counseling with the Chamberses called for an approach which would help them gain insight into the needs and expectancies each brought to the other, but which would also allow Linda and Tom to develop a relationship of mutuality based on personhood instead of roles.

To help Linda gain more awareness of herself as a person, she wrote a daily journal in which she recorded her thoughts and feelings. These could be shared with Tom if she wished. She was also asked by the pastor to write an autobiography describing significant people and events in her life. In counseling sessions, the autobiography was used both as a vehicle for insight into the ways she tended to interact with other people and as a resource for self-discovery. (The autobiography revealed a keen interest in art, which had gone unnoticed in her own family's financial struggle. Later, Linda picked up this interest and even enrolled in an extension course on modern art.)

Pastor Ames introduced assertive training[5] to help Linda gain more autonomy. Since she tended to wait for cues from others and then accommodate, assertive training provided opportunities for Linda to be active instead of reactive, to practice expression of *her* feelings and wishes in her relationships with others.

The pastor gave assignments in small steps, beginning with simple forms of assertion and then gradually moving to situations

---

5. Assertive training is a form of behavioral therapy in which the counselee is encouraged to risk self-expression. The assertive actions are done in carefully graduated steps to ensure counselee success at each point until self-confidence is established. (Arnold A. Lazarus, *Behavior Therapy and Beyond* [New York: McGraw-Hill, 1971], pp. 115–40.)

which involved risk of disapproval. A beginning assignment for Linda was to plan evening meals to include the foods that she liked, instead of asking Tom each night what he wanted. Together, she and Pastor Ames developed a hierarchy of situations which involved increasing degrees of self-assertion until a later assignment required her to complain to the supermarket manager about a stale loaf of bread she had purchased.

In discussion of these assignments, Linda began to shift the locus of self-valuation from others to herself. Using the methodology of rational-emotive psychotherapy, she learned to analyze her feelings of rejection in a variety of situations. She discovered that disapproval by others (point A) led to a sense of rejection and unworth (point C) due to her interpretation at point B: To be a worthwhile person, to be a good Christian, I should please everyone all the time.[6] Pastor Ames's insistence that the gospel communicated acceptance for her and freedom in Christ to be a person led to the insight that self-giving presupposes and involves a genuine self, not a mirror image of others.

For Tom, counseling took a different course. Pastor Ames gave him assignments in sensitivity training,[7] first asking him to listen for the feeling behind Linda's words, then to respond with concern for those feelings. He was encouraged to identify his own feelings in various situations and put them into words. Another assignment required him to make statements of appreciation rather than approval. ("I enjoyed the dinner" as opposed to "You cooked a good dinner.") Along with discussion, sensitivity

6. The A-B-C method of rational-emotive psychotherapy is used to uncover irrational beliefs held by the counselee. Point A is the activating event; point B is the belief system of the counselee which produced point C, the emotional consequence. The counselee usually sees point A as producing point C, when point B—what the counselee tells himself about point A—actually produces point C. (Albert Ellis, *Growth through Reason* [Palo Alto, Calif.: Science and Behavior Books, 1971]; Paul A. Hauck, *Reason in Pastoral Counseling* [Philadelphia: Westminster Press, 1972].)

7. Sensitivity training is a form of behavioral therapy used to aid the counselee in learning habits of emotional freedom which include expressions of love, affection, and appreciation, as well as appropriate expression of frustration and anger. Assignments are given by the counselor which help the counselee become aware of his own feelings and gain sensitivity to the emotions of others. (Lazarus, *Behavior Therapy and Beyond*, pp. 115–40.)

assignments opened the way for reexamination by Tom of the connection he had made between tight emotional control and masculine strength. He began to discover a new dimension to strength as he allowed himself to experience his own full range of emotions as well as Linda's.

As a pastoral counselor, Ames could, legitimately, have dealt with Linda's immediate personal crisis and assumed an understanding but passive stance toward the marriage relationship itself. But this approach would have been to counsel adjustment to a role structure likely to produce similar episodes of unhappiness and guilt in the future. Pastor Ames chose instead an active counseling approach that would allow Christian values to be actualized in the Chamberses' marriage. His approach involved sorting out, cognitively, the confusion of Christianity with a social model of feminine-masculine role behavior. And the distilled Christian emphases—growth of persons and mutuality between husband and wife—needed to be translated emotionally and behaviorally in the counseling process.

The role of women has undergone more changes in the last several decades than any other role in our society. The changes are often as difficult for men as they are for women. But in the midst of change, the resurgence of the affirmative biblical-theological tradition gives promise of renewing that which the early Christian movement offered—new hope and new life for both men and women.

5. Human Sexuality
Outside the Coupled World

"So here I am, after eight years of marriage and two children —and a husband who walked out on me." The words are familiar to every pastoral counselor; they vary only in the details of the particular situation. Joanne Tyler is 29 years old and has been divorced for six months. Now she is working again, as a secretary-bookkeeper, to supplement the small alimony payments mailed to her monthly. Her bitterness toward her former husband is clear. Not so evident are her feelings of rejection and of mistrust of all men. Despite these feelings, she admits that her ultimate goal is to marry again. "I know that sounds strange after all the things I've just said. But after you've been married, somehow that still seems to be the best thing. And I guess that's what I'll eventually be." Until she does get married, however, some life style adjustments need to be made. And concern over them is what brings her to the pastor. "How can I be both mother and father to my children and still be myself as an adult in my own world? And, you know, it's very strange, somehow—I'm single again, and suddenly I don't seem to fit." It is, of course, the problem faced by single persons in a coupled world, a world which classifies and understands adults primarily in terms of married couples. And whether the person is involuntarily single or divorced, a widow or a widower, or, as is increasingly the case in contemporary society, one who simply chooses to live as a single with no immediate plans for marriage—whatever the reason, the difficulties for a single person in a coupled world are many.

Jane Reynolds is thirty-two years old, a graduate of a two-year school of fashion design and interior decorating. She graduated when she was twenty, worked for two years as a window decorator in a department store in Boston, and then took a position as an assistant buyer of women's wear in a large department store in the South. She has, in the ensuing years, become the chief buyer for the store as well as for one other store in the chain. Increasingly, her age and her job orientation have limited her social contacts and she moves about in a world that has no structured way of including her. She finds her social life unsatisfactory because most of her friends are married, and as a single she feels out of place in events planned for couples.

For Jane, one point of contact with others beyond her work has been the church. While not particularly religious, she finds that the church meets aesthetic and ethical needs within a community setting. Even here, however, she senses that while there is recognition of single persons, the social activity appears to concentrate either on singles in late adolescence or on those who are widowed and much older.

While Jane feels some sexual tensions and even, at times, twinges of domesticity and maternity, these are low on her scale of needs. What she does need and seek is relationship with others in a more than superficial manner and, somehow, somewhere, a place in a coupled world that will recognize her value as a person without expressions of puzzled concern or implicit expectations concerning her single status.

Jonathan Bell is thirty years old, a certified public accountant with an insurance company, and appears to be reserved and scholarly. He has a small group of male friends with whom he has a good relationship and, in addition, he periodically dates several women. The pastor's previous contacts with him indicate that, while Jonathan has no objections to marriage, he is in no hurry to get married and does have some strong feelings against being considered an eligible bachelor. Recently, however, he has been dating a young female attorney with regularity and some friends suspect that he is beginning to think seriously about marriage.

At this point, he comes to the pastor of his church in order to discuss an important matter. To the surprise of the pastor, who

had anticipated a discussion about marriage, Jonathan quickly
says that the young woman has no marriage aspirations and, in
fact, would view marriage in the next few years as a "cop-out"
on her professional career. The heart of the discussion appears in
the following dialogue:

Jonathan: What really creates the problem for me is the fact that I find
   Dorothy increasingly attractive as a person and I enjoy being with her
   very much.
Pastor: And this is leading *you* toward thinking of marriage? . . . wishing
   that she. . . .
Jonathan: Oh, no—not that. I'm not ready to think in those terms and
   certainly Dorothy has made that clear. But . . . well, she . . . we
   recognize certain things that might occur in the future and . . . .
Pastor: Such as . . . .
Jonathan: Well, we are attracted to each other, enjoy each other's company and, sooner or later I guess, we're going to have to face the
   possibility of sex.
Pastor: Hmmm . . . and this is the problem you referred to?
Jonathan: Yes, it is. And I'm not quite sure how to view it. Oh, that isn't
   quite true; I don't see anything wrong with it—maybe you do—but I'm
   just trying to work it all out in my mind.
   I guess what I'm really asking is: If we do care for each other—and
   we do—is sexual expression of this caring legitimate even though we
   have no plans for marriage? . . . haven't even considered marriage . . .
   or, well, to be frank, is it just a kind of sophisticated fornication? . . .
   and am I hunting an excuse . . . I don't think I . . . we are . . . well,
   that's about it. What do you think?

Being single in a coupled world is not easy. And the task of the
counselor is to attempt in each case to understand how the problem presents itself to the particular individual and to help that
individual arrive at the best possible solution. Without this focus
on the individual problem and solution, the temptation will always be present for the counselor to urge marriage as an ultimate
solution. In the cases of Jane and Jonathan it should be clear that
marriage as a solution is precisely what they have rejected. They
ask to be regarded as normal, functioning human beings within
their role as single individuals.

The immediate task of the pastor, then, is to ascertain where the counselee stands with regard to his particular problem, that is, how he perceives the difficulties involved in being single and how much effort he is willing to exert in coping with the problem. There are varied ways to approach the problem of the single person but to a great extent the success of the particular approach is contingent upon the effort and willingness of the individual to work with the counselor on that approach. While a certain amount of consciousness-raising may occur within the counselee, it is unlikely that the counseling pastor will be able to move toward a solution which exceeds to any great degree the perimeters of the counselee's own understanding of the situation and desire to deal with it.

Focusing on the Individual

Further discussion with Joanne Tyler fills in the details of her present situation. Her former husband, owner-operator of a gasoline station, deserted her a year and a half ago, overwhelmed, as he said, with long hours, hard work, and too many demands. The second child, a two-year-old girl, was wanted, but not so soon. Joanne's recurring illnesses following the birth of the child prevented her from continuing to help her husband with his book work at the gasoline station. Her failure to help led to feelings of guilt about the part she had played in making her husband's position intolerable for him. In addition, the fact of the divorce itself was guilt-producing, bringing her feelings of unworthiness and causing her to question her competence for the future.

The question for the pastor is where to begin with Joanne. In point of fact, there are three options open to him: The first is the past, highlighted by the divorce and its production of guilt. The second is the present, with her adjustments to being father-mother-adult and single. The third is the future, with the establishment of goals and the development of a personhood capable of moving into the future with a renewed sense of self. The decision between the three needs to be based on an estimate of therapeutic gain: At what point of entry into the situation will the gain be most immediate? Perhaps it would be advantageous to start at the combination point of the present-future options, dealing eventually with the past as a subsidiary, but very important, option. There is always the temptation for the counseling pastor to start with the option most comfortable and familiar for him: the past with its divorce and guilt. But to do so would be to overlook Joanne's statement of the presenting problem—"How can I be both mother and father . . . and adult . . . and I'm single again . . . ?—and her struggle to meet the requirements of family living in the present. The pastor, therefore, begins at the point of her greatest need; her immediate life style becomes the target for his work.

The Counselor's Relationship and Modeling Role

As the pastor moves into the present-future option, he is aware of the fundamental importance of the relationship and modeling role in which he is involved. Joanne holds feelings of anger, resentment, and mistrust toward all men, generalized from her direct feelings toward her former husband and his desertion of her. The fact that the pastor now must serve as a model for male behavior becomes crucial. Not only are his attitudes, which she will discern, important, but the day by day encounters are equally important. He must be accepting of her and concerned for her and, most of all, steady in his dealings with her. For example, to miss an appointment or to change a scheduled appointment could signal a lack of real concern to a person such as Joanne (deserted again?). The counselor may be a busy and involved pastor, but that is not the impression she would receive. She would see only the picture of another undependable man.

Yet, in his modeling, the pastor needs to be honest enough to admit his own failings and not assume a perfectionist role. It is important to be open and to explain and, thus, to achieve gradually her acceptance of the failings and problems of others. While all of this relationship development and modeling carries the undergirding theological implications of acceptance and forgiveness, it is best not to mention this corollary until well toward the termination of counseling, unless Joanne brings it up. To speak of it too soon will be to suggest that the counselor is more a professional interested in his theology than a genuine human being concerned for Joanne and her problems.

As the relationship deepens, it might be helpful for the counselor—if his own married life is warm and accepting—to invite Joanne to his home for an evening of routine activity and talk. Once again, this should be done close to the termination stage of counseling rather than at the beginning. If done too soon, it will simply reinforce her sense of loss and increase her sense of isolation as a single person in a happily coupled world.

The Problem of Being Single Again

In working with Joanne in the present-future aspect of her situation, the pastor will need to deal with the problem of being single again. Joanne expressed the feelings she was having when she said, "And you know, it's very strange, somehow—I'm single again, and suddenly I don't seem to fit."

There are basically three possible approaches to the problems of a single person in contemporary society: first, adjusting the single to the situation; second, attempting to change those elements within the single situation which are amenable to change; third, moving toward what might be called the "imponderable new." To be sure, the lines between the three are blurred and indecisive. Actually there is a continuum on which the varied solution-points may arbitrarily be indicated. Nevertheless, to see them as separate approaches is helpful for purposes of clarity.

The first possibility, that of making an accepting adjustment to the coupled world, may appear to be no solution whatever to the problem of the single person. Yet it is, in fact, a type of solution which many singles have arrived at and are living with at the present time. In essence, this option implies one of two alternatives: either learn to be content with singleness and its problems or move to marriage. In hearing Joanne's discussion of her situation and her suggestion of eventual marriage, it would appear that adjustment to the present and working toward future marriage would be the central thrust for the pastor to follow in his work with her. But whether or not this is a happy solution to any single's problem is increasingly becoming a moot question and must be so viewed by the pastoral counselor.

At this point in the counseling of Joanne the discussion of sex roles in Chapter 4 becomes useful. Without attempting to interfere with her future hope of marriage, it is most important that the counselor spend time on Joanne's development as a person, quite apart from her possible future as a wife and even her present as a mother. Without an understanding of herself as a valuable person in her own right, she will tend, in the event of future marriage, to lose her identity once again in roles which depend largely upon other people for their meaning. Therefore, assertive training coupled with readings to be discussed with the counselor would be helpful. Reading what others are saying will help to diminish her feelings of isolation as she moves toward a new view of herself. It will also give her confidence as she changes her circle of friends, loosening the bonds to former "couple-friends" and forming new bonds to other friends around her.

Dealing with the Divorce

The pastor is aware of the importance of dealing with the divorce even though his counseling emphasis at the beginning was on the present-future aspects of Joanne's life. Not only were the desertion and consequent divorce the precipitating factors in Joanne's present situation, but their subsidiary effects have important continuing consequences for her present and future life. Having deliberately chosen to deal with present-future possibilities, the counselor needs now to deal with the divorce too, lest it become an unresolved area of her life.

The pastor is aware that, whatever the church may say theologically about forgiveness and the new life, its members in fact tend to implant and reinforce guilt feelings in anyone who, for whatever reason, participates in the disintegration of a marriage relationship. On the one hand, this is done subtly by the average church's emphasis on family life in its program, little or no provision being made for those who are single. On the other hand, guilt feelings are aroused by the theological importance attached to marriage and the implied failure in those who are partners to a broken marriage.

The biblical and theological background, despite attempts to circumvent or soften it, is rigid and unyielding: divorce is either impossible (Mark 10:2-12; Luke 16:18) or admissible only on grounds of adultery (Matt. 5:32). The traditional marriage ceremony reinforces this strict view: "till death us do part" promise the participants. Prejudice even against digamy (remarriage after the death of one's spouse) has roots in the apostolic period and comes to fruition in the church of the second century. For varying reasons the divorce rate in the United States has risen sharply in recent decades and, consequently, created a wider public acceptance of divorce. But despite current moods in society, the counseling pastor needs to be aware of the tradition in which he stands and the effect of that tradition upon the church. The translation of this tradition into contemporary life becomes important for people in Joanne's situation.

Despite the cynicism surrounding some publicity-ridden marriages and the intent of the participants, it seems appropriate to believe that the vast majority of individuals do promise and intend a lifelong commitment at the time of their marriage. But given the pressures of contemporary life as well as the varied elements of past and future personal development on the part of the participants, it becomes apparent to the counselor that promises sincerely made are always made by fallible human beings. When uncompromising emphasis is placed upon the promise, the institution of marriage is elevated above the people who comprise the institution. And, ironically, it is this very valuing of institutions above persons that Jesus opposed with some passion throughout the Gospels.

The affirmation of the individual becomes the important point for the pastoral counselor, the point at which his heritage has a meeting place with contemporary thought. This affirmation is found in the forgiveness proferred to all who are involved in human sin, the recognition that man can be *simul justus et peccator,* simultaneously justified and sinner. On this view sin and transgression are taken seriously, they are not condoned, while at the same time institutions and the attitudes toward them are kept free from juridical casuistry. Thus, from a Christian viewpoint a lifelong marriage is indeed that which is promised, hoped for, and worked toward; but the institution is not, in the face of irreconcilable difficulties, that which must be preserved inviolate at whatever cost to the individuals concerned.

Realistic and Unrealistic Guilt

The guilt which Joanne feels about her broken marriage should be viewed by the pastor as both real and appropriate. To be sure, her husband deserted her and she appears to be more sinned against than sinning. But most people, certainly all counselors, are aware of the total involvement of both parties in any marriage breakdown. And Joanne knows that promises were made when vows were exchanged. This realistic guilt, handled carefully by the counselor, can be amenable to the forgiveness of God.

There is an unrealistic guilt present also which the pastor needs to recognize and deal with in Joanne's situation. This is the guilt which she feels for discontinuing her help to her husband following the birth of their second child during her protracted illness. This guilt is self-instilled and strikes at her view of herself as a viable human being.

One method of dealing with such unrealistic guilt is that provided by rational-emotive psychotherapy with its emphasis on approaching feelings by way of rational thought. One segment of a counseling episode reveals both the method and Joanne's reaction to it.

Joanne: I know it may not be correct but I can't help feeling that it was my sickness which led to my husband's feelings of being overworked.
Pastor: So that you couldn't help him and it all became just too much.
Joanne: Yes, that's it—and I can't help feeling . . . .

Pastor: All right, let's look at that a minute. You were sick and obviously you couldn't help that . . . .

Joanne: No, I couldn't. I had to see the doctor almost daily for awhile and I just . . . .

Pastor: So then it was a fact that you were sick and no matter what you might have wanted to do, you had little choice in the matter. Now where does the guilt come in?

Joanne: Well . . . I guess, at what I failed to do . . . I just feel . . . .

Pastor: Now wait a minute. Let's look at this. A—you were sick and under a doctor's care. OK? Now, skip B and go to C—"My husband left me and I feel guilty about my part in it." Now point C should be the result of A, right? But it just doesn't follow: plenty of wives get sick and plenty of husbands leave their wives and there's no connection between the two.

Therefore, you must be telling yourself something about the fact that you were sick and your husband left you that is causing the guilt—and that we call point B. Now what could that be?

Joanne: I think I follow you, but I'm kind of confused—point B—I just don't know . . . .

Pastor: All right, let me try: A—you were sick and under a doctor's care; B—"But I *should not* be sick and I *should always* be able to help my husband. I *should be* a perfect wife. And since I am not, I must be worthless and no man would want to stay with me." Now add C—"My husband left me and I feel guilty about my part in it."

Joanne: Oh, I see—let me think about that a minute . . . what you're saying is that I got sick and that was all right. But I demanded perfection of myself and when I could not find it, I took the next step and said that this was why my husband left me . . . .

Pastor: Right—and that's why you felt guilty: not really because you were sick but because you felt you should be perfect . . . And remember what we said some time before: We're always both saint and sinner, and to call for perfection is to ignore our humanness . . . .

Joanne: Yes, I do see that . . . maybe I was not perfect . . . but then, no one is . . . I think I see that now.

Counselors often find it valuable when using this approach in counseling to take a sheet of paper and write out items A and C and then, while discussing them, fill in B. It helps the counselee to actually look at the sentences as well as hear them. This sheet of paper may be given to the counselee to take along and examine. As a homework assignment, he may even be asked to put

Jonathan points up the issue in unmistakable terms: "Well, we are attracted to each other, enjoy each other's company and, sooner or later I guess, we're going to have to face the possibility of sex." He is speaking about his developing friendship with a young woman who, like himself, does not have marriage as a goal: "I guess what I'm really asking is: If we do care for each other—and we do—is sexual expression of this caring legitimate even though we have no plans for marriage? . . . What do you think?"

The pastor recognizes that the issue is broader than simply that of genital sex expression. The choice of being single carries with it the major hazard of limiting one's opportunity for continuing personal growth through close interpersonal relationships. While questions may be raised about the interpretations given to the studies, research indicates that being a single adult in contemporary society carries with it both psychological and physiological problems. Not only does the single adult find it difficult to locate a place for himself in a coupled world but, perhaps more serious, he is shunted by this difficulty into the negative aspect of young adult development described by Erik Erikson as the polarization of intimacy and isolation.[3] That this will lead to problems in the later developmental stage of generativity versus stagnation is not inevitable, but they may well occur.[4] The point is this: Crucial to the development of the single adult are intimate relationships, relationships which deal with the totality of human personality including sexuality.

So Jonathan comes to the pastor for help in facing the full potential of a developing relationship with a young woman which does not carry any evident prospects for marriage. In the view of both church and society, Jonathan's case does not fit a premarital

3. Erik Erikson, "Growth and Crises of the Healthy Personality," *Psychological Issues,* ed. George S. Klein (New York: International Universities Press, 1959).
4. Erikson sees a struggle in midlife between the more mature expression of generativity in the person as opposed to stagnation, boredom, and interpersonal impoverishment. (Erik H. Erikson, *Identity: Youth and Crises* [New York: W. W. Norton and Co., 1968], pp. 138–39.)

category. It is rather, simply and clearly, a case of two singles in a relationship of developing intimacy—two consenting adults.

The counselor, in his conversation with Jonathan, has already received some insight into his counselee's viewpoint: "I don't see anything wrong with it—maybe you do—but I'm just trying to work it all out in my mind."

Yet even as he says this Jonathan obviously has some nagging feeling that prompts him to seek help in working through his thinking about the situation. In essence, Jonathan seems to be saying, "There may be something in all this that I don't see. If there is, I want you to tell me about it so that I can weigh it in as part of my thinking."

Subdividing the Options in a Relationship

The counseling pastor may find it helpful at this point to subdivide the varying possibilities within such a relationship and examine each option in turn: first, an intimate relationship with no sexual expression; second, an intimate relationship with limited sexual expression; third, an intimate relationship with full sexual expression. In each of these three subdivisions or options the fact of an intimate relationship is accepted. Obviously, a man and a woman in contemporary society, both single, may have a dating relationship which becomes exclusive. Such exclusiveness is both important and healthy for personal development. The problem arises when the possibility of sexual intimacy appears in the relationship. Thus, the variable to be considered is not primarily the relationship itself but the increasing amount of sexual expression and the effects which this may have on the relationship.

An intimate relationship with no sexual expression is the model held by society and the church as the norm for engaged couples and single young adults. In this model the tie between celibacy and singleness is intact and any deviation from this norm is expected to be in the direction of marriage. (". . . if they cannot control themselves, they should marry. Better be married than burn with vain desire" [1 Cor. 7:8–9].) In the case of Jonathan and his friend, however, there is no evident desire for marriage, for reasons they consider to be compelling and legitimate. Despite the model, society appears to observe this kind of intimate relationship devoid of sexual expression more in the breach than in fact.[5] With a changing social climate that allows for freer discussion, what has been clandestine about this model over the years is today out in the open. Furthermore, the availability of contraceptive aids, while it does not necessarily create, certainly allows a reasonably safe sexual expression outside a marriage contract.

The church still holds to the model of singleness and celibacy, though positions vary from explicit endorsement to questions without answers. So some denominations state unequivocally that sexual intercourse outside the context of the marriage union is morally wrong, to which others respond by asking if all that can be offered to the single adult, then, is repression or abstinence.[6] The counseling pastor discovers that the church's viewpoint is basically legalistic, with no allowance for special questions in individual situations. The same view—no sex outside of marriage—is held for an unsophisticated, immature fifteen-year-old boy as for a highly educated, mature individual thirty years of age. Such an approach might be valid if there were an incisive dictum from the biblical-theological heritage representative of the best of that tradition. There is, however, no such clear-cut dictum, and the attempt of both society and the church to draw lines at a legalistic position is as doomed to failure in the future as it has been in the past. Gone today are reasons which once spoke for holding back:

> There was a young lady named Wilde
> Who kept herself quite undefiled

5. Robert R. Bell, *Premarital Sex in a Changing Society* (Englewood Cliffs, N.J.: Prentice-Hall, 1966).
6. For a review of several denominational positions on the single person, see Chapter 3, "The Single Person—A New Species of Human," Robert T. Francoeur, *Eve's New Rib* (New York: Harcourt Brace Jovanovich, 1972).

By thinking of Jesus
And social diseases
And the fear of having a child.[7]

But the pastor can present to Jonathan a viewpoint more representative of the affirmative biblical-theological tradition. This viewpoint, not new but still valid, asks for an assessment on the basis of whether or not *this* is the moment, the time, and the particular relationship in which a sexual response is to be made. To make a sexual response without considering these questions is either to be victimized by an unquestioned drive or to act in the present without consideration of the future. This is not to overvalue or undervalue virginity or chastity, but simply to ask about the appropriate time to invest it.

To consider the relationship of these two single adults from the viewpoint of the future as well as the present is to avoid a legalism which denies sexual expression without considering its meaning within the totality of relationship. Furthermore, to acknowledge sexuality as part of the total consideration gives credence to the unity of the person, avoiding the spirit-matter dualism which otherwise creeps so easily into Christian thought. To disconnect the sexual aspects of man from an intimate relationship, as legalistic codes attempt to do, is to imply that such separation is a proper and adequate mode of life even though it ignores the goodness of the totality of life as God created it.

The question at this stage of consideration becomes: Is this the relationship, the time, and the setting in which the totality of self is to be invested? If the answer is no, then the matter has reached a conclusion for Jonathan. If the answer is yes, or a possible yes, then the pastoral counselor moves with Jonathan into a consideration of further options.

The second subdivision or option to be considered is an intimate relationship with limited sexual expression. Discussion of this option requires a definition of the word "limited," and such

7. Tom McGinnis, article in *Marital Therapy*, ed. H. L. Silverman (Springfield, Ill.: Charles C. Thomas, 1972), p. 109.

definition ultimately belongs to the counselee rather than the counselor. Obviously, limited sexual expression appears to exclude sexual intercourse; but given that exclusion, the concept of a limited expression goes anywhere from the minimal body contact of holding hands to petting leading to orgasm.

The traditional biblical-theological base for this approach to sexuality is the emphasis on virginity as a sublime condition for men and women. Since no intermediate concept such as petting appears in the Old or New Testaments, the thought about sexual expression is dichotomized: virgin or nonvirgin; coitus or no coitus. Paul's approach is favorable to the concept of celibacy and virginity; this is based, however, not on the intrinsic virtues of such a condition but on Paul's eschatological worldview which pushed toward a status quo "until the Lord comes." Only in later Augustinian thought does the attitude crystallize to the point where sexual acts outside of coitus are condemned as sinful.

The major difficulty in espousing an intimate relationship with limited sexual expression is the implicit view that the act of intercourse is the *sine qua non* of all sexual relationships. Not only does intercourse serve as a definition of sexual relationship, but sexual expression without intercourse also appears to be viewed as different in both kind and degree. To be sure, legalism needs a focus point, and sexual intercourse serves that need. But in selecting such a point, legalism creates what many writers call "technical virgins": men and women who have had wide orgasmic experience but who have refrained from the act of inserting the penis into the vagina. By such avoidance the law is fulfilled—but hardly observed!

Jesus' insistence on the primacy of motivation and thought as opposed to act (the method he used to correct the legalism of his day) is still an important corrective to a legalistic viewpoint. It is this insistence that takes a negative approach to sexuality and, in translating it into actual situations, makes it affirmative.

If the intent of the individuals involved is for a totality of relationship, then whether or not coitus occurs becomes a matter for decision about that act, or any other act, by the couple, rather than a question of subordinate steps leading to a supreme act. This viewpoint is sometimes overlooked because limited sexual expression is, as any counselor knows, a prevailing practice in adolescent boy-girl relationships. The fact of its connection with adolescence tends to convey, as a result, an implication of its being an immature practice.

The counseling pastor would do well to indicate to Jonathan that, however the counselee views this option, there *is* depth of meaning which limited sexual expression will have within an intimate relationship. In saying this, the pastor indicates the limitations set by an affirmative view of sexuality; for if there is deep meaning in these acts short of coitus, then they should not be utilized in careless fashion. Furthermore, such acts are not seen responsibly as simply preliminary steps toward something more significant.

The third subdivision or option, an intimate relationship with full sexual expression, comes into reasonable existence with the increasing medical knowledge about contraception. Throughout the centuries, the connection of coitus with procreation has created numerous strands of influence in the matter of human sexuality, from a desire for certainty in family lines to the view of women as property in marriage. Such a connection helped to create the double standard in sexual expression for men, in that the one escape from procreation, and hence the only point at which sex moved from hazardous duty to entertainment, was coitus outside the marriage relationship.

Since the question of coitus and procreation loses its meaning in the face of effective contraception, the pastoral counselor perceives that the major restriction on coitus has disappeared. The issue of morality is both misunderstood and misplaced if coitus itself is made the center of debate. This is, once again, to impose a legalism at a point where it cannot be maintained. Sexuality has many intimate forms and to suggest that intercourse is more intimate than other forms is to add a mysticism to the act which is neither understood nor observed by contemporary man. The manifold dysfunctions of human sexuality which are increasingly being aired in public discussion clearly indicate that human sexuality is a total expression of the total personality rather than a simplistic subdivision involving many small steps and functions.

The Requirements of Intimate Relationship

The fundamental issue, therfore, in speaking with Jonathan about an intimate relationship with full sexual expression, is the relationship itself. The movement in the counseling process should be toward defining and examining the relationship between the two persons which becomes crucial because of their potentially total involvement with each other.

A primary consideration is the psychological competence —maturity—of the individuals involved in a relationship to set limits within that relationship and then move beyond them by agreement.[8] Only a maturity that seeks a communion within a relationship, rather than merely an orgasmic or individual experience, is able to use the totality of sexual expression in an enhancing fashion. Intimacy has threatening as well as fulfilling aspects for the individual, and to deepen intimacy without an acceptance of its total meaning will be destructive to the goal itself. What the pastoral counselor says at this point is therefore as pertinent for a couple within a marriage contract as it is for Jonathan and his friend.

The pastor considers intimate relationship and suggests four criteria as necessary for its development and for any assessment of it. The type of love involved is the beginning point. Even apart from sexual expression, love as *agape* must be present if the relationship is to be a serving as well as a served one.

Closely akin to love, different only in degree, is the element of genuine concern. The relationship should be developed enough to meet individual needs, but not at the expense of exploitation. Thus, freedom is granted in those areas of the relationship where

8. It is developmental maturity rather than negativism alone which indicates why early adolescence is not an appropriate time for unlimited sexual expression. See Herbert W. Richardson, *Nun, Witch, Playmate* (New York: Harper and Row, 1971), chap. 7.

restrictions and demands are inappropriate and purely self-serving.

Third, responsibility is necessary in an intimate relationship. To allow a pregnancy to occur, for example, without mutual a-greement and plans for the future is to negate the benefits desired in such a relationship by dealing carelessly with its demands.

Finally, a commitment by both parties to each other and the relationship is necessary if the relationship is to develop and deepen through time. Certainly its design is not in the nature of a legal marriage commitment. But it can have the nature of a uniquely freeing commitment in the sense that it is open to and bent upon the future growth and well-being of each of the partners.

As the pastor reviews these elements of a meaningful intimate relationship, it is evident to him—and to Jonathan—that what is being described is in substance the equivalent of a marriage relationship. Everything is present in what Jonathan is contemplating except a license, a ceremony, and living together in one place, although even that may occur. Intimate relationship without marriage does not escape the requirements of intimate relationship with marriage. In fact, it imposes one additional burden, beyond the lack of legal niceties: the loss of corporate and public recognition of the relationship. To live in intimate relationship without being able to acknowledge it openly may pose a heavy burden. Even more, it may lose for that relationship the wider aspects of friendship and social intermingling which could enrich both parties.

Whatever life style Jonathan and his friend may finally opt for, the pastor will work with them, hopefully with both of them together, to aid them in arriving at a responsible decision. The result may be a life style foreign to him and to most members of his congregation. "But," the pastor says to himself as they leave, "what makes a marriage? A legal document—love—a promise—a relationship—or all of them?" He has learned to ask this hard question also of every couple coming to him to be married.

6. The Counseling Pastor and Expectations

A major crisis occurs for a pastor when he feels compelled to take a viewpoint quite opposite from that which is representative of his congregation. When such crises are examined, it becomes apparent that the difficulty lies not just in the differing viewpoints on the matter itself but in the differing expectations that his members—and he—have about the pastor's role or roles. James E. Dittes explains:

> Perhaps the most annoying, persistent, and handicapping resistance which a minister faces is the difference between his and his laymen's expectations of what his role should be—what he as minister should do and how he should do it. Or to put it as he more likely feels it, the problem is their misinterpretation of his role. On the basis of his professional training and his own sense of call, the minister feels some direction and conviction about how he should proceed—which of the myriad possible ministerial activities are most urgent, and how each should be carried out. But the laymen to whom he would minister are likely to have equally firm expectations which are not necessarily consistent with his. In fact, they have *hired* him.[1]

While always a source of difficulty, expectancies and role-confusion can usually be lived with if pastor and people are mutually accepting of one another. When, however, the issue separating the two is charged with strong emotion and potential conflict, mutual acceptance breaks down. Human sexuality frequently proves to be such an issue.

A Case of Crisis

Pastor Mark Stewart angrily tapped the edge of the envelope against the top of his desk. The letter he had just finished reading

1. James E. Dittes, *The Church in the Way* (New York: Charles Scribner's Sons, 1967), p. 276.

was anonymous. It was the third such letter he had received in the past ten days and each dealt with the same subject: an accusation of homosexuality against one of the official church board members. But the letters were intended to be more than accusatory. Each letter carried the same threat: "Remove John Harper from the board or there will be a scandal. It is your duty to save the church."

John Harper, thirty-three years old, was single, secretary of the church board, and active in church and civic affairs. He was assistant manager of a paint store and instrumental in creating for the store a highly profitable trade in artists' supplies. Although quiet, he was quite popular in the church with many of the members. "And now this," thought the pastor. "Poor John."

The letters didn't really surprise Stewart, although he was concerned about the threats. He had heard rumors about Harper, and one of his church board members had spoken to him in confidence about the rumors he also had heard. But there was nothing concrete, only anonymous letters with threats and rumors—a worrisome situation but, at the present, veiled. The pastor hoped it would stay that way and eventually die down. But it didn't.

The next week, following an official board meeting, five board members came to the pastor and asked to discuss a personal matter. The subject was John Harper. All of the men were concerned about the rumors, but one man insisted that his information was more than hearsay. A professional friend of his from Washington, D.C., who had contact with the gay world there, passed word along that John Harper, identified through a traffic violation, was with the homosexual community. Moreover, he'd been with the community on numerous occasions. At least once a month Harper went to Washington for several days. The trips were made for business purposes, but his social activities seemed to center on homosexual contacts. After some discussion, the board members asked that the pastor speak to Harper about the rumors and discuss with him the best method of handling the situation.

The pastor left the informal meeting in puzzlement. He wasn't

quite certain what they expected of him. Certainly talking to
Harper about the rumors was clear enough. But what did they
mean by the "best method of handling the situation"? When the
pastor got home, he called one of the five to try to clarify his
assignment.

Pastor: Roy, I got the rumor part of the assignment clear enough, but
what did you all mean about the best method of handling it? Did you
mean how to handle the rumors?
Roy: Well, certainly that. We've got to spike all this talk. But there's
more to it than that . . . uh, we talked a bit before we came in to see
you. We weren't quite certain how you would take it, but . . . well,
perhaps if you talk to John and it's not true, or he'll change, then we
can work it out. But if he is a homosexual and, you know, sticks to it
. . . well, then for the good of the church—and John—we think you
should ask him to resign.
Pastor: . . . ask him to resign? I'm not at all sure of that. To be honest, I
don't know too much about homosexuality, in the technical sense, that
is . . . .
Roy: That's not the point. I don't know much about it either, but I don't
like it, and, well . . . there'll be hell to pay if it's proven and he stays
on the official board. You've got to be firm about this, pastor. Either
he says it's not true—and can prove it—or he changes, or he must go.
And I think if you're wise, you'll be firm.

Attitudes toward Homosexuality

The next morning Pastor Stewart decided to do some research
on homosexuality. Three sources were important for his study:
the behavioral sciences, the biblical-theological tradition of the
church, and contemporary statements by the church on this subject. Using information from these sources, he hoped to come to
some conclusions about homosexuality. He realized that he
seemed to be working on the assumption that Harper was indeed
homosexual, which might not be true. But he needed background
knowledge before he could even attempt a conference with John.

From the behavioral sciences he discovered that 4 to 6 percent
of the American population is homosexual and that during
adolescence most males have homosexual experiences which do
not lead to adult homosexuality. While many possible influences

are suggested, there appears to be no definitive cause for the development of homosexuality. Further, Stewart discovered that the possibilities for therapeutic help are limited, with recent behavioral aversion methods[2] apparently the most successful. Professional therapists show ambiguity in their viewpoints on homosexuality, varying from the one extreme of complete acceptance and defense of its normality to the other extreme of defining it as a sickness and a sexual deviation. As Pastor Stewart continued reading, he remembered the tension of his seminary days when the students discovered one of their fellow students to be a homosexual. The arguments flowed, camps were formed, but no conclusions were reached. The picture, somehow, was as indecisive today.

Homosexuality in the biblical-theological tradition was viewed as a deviate style of life, mainly because of the emphasis on heterosexuality as the norm and proper order of creation. When the subject was dealt with at all—and this was limited—it was usually as an indictment of, and a defense against, the pagan cultures surrounding the Christians. Thus Paul in the first chapter of Romans says that these pagan cultures know God but refuse to obey him. "In consequence . . . God has given them up to shameful passions . . . . their men in turn, giving up natural relations with women, burn with lust for one another; males behave indecently with males, and are paid in their own persons the fitting wage of such perversion" (Rom. 1:26–27). Contemporary church statements on homosexuality are diversified, ranging from cautious acceptance on the one hand to outright condemnation on the other hand. Without exception, they deplore the manner in which society treats the homosexual by oppressive laws and dis-

2. Aversion therapy is a method penalizing a reaction to a stimulus in contrast to ignoring or rewarding the reaction. An electric shock is an example of an aversive device. The purpose of aversion therapy is to drive a behavioral response to extinction. Aversion therapy, as in all forms of behavior therapy, is never done without the full knowledge and consent of the counselee. (Stanley Rachman and John Teasdale, *Aversion Therapy and Behavior Disorders: An Analysis* [Coral Gables, Fla.: University of Miami Press, 1969].)

criminatory practices. Further, the statements all urge acceptance of the homosexual as a person, apart from his homosexuality.

It seemed to Stewart, as he thought about it, that homosexuality was not a life style selected by an individual any more than heterosexuality is a life style choice. Choice—freedom to choose—seemed to have little to do with the subject. Developmental influences and, perhaps, genetic backgrounds created the condition. Thus, homosexuality as a condition is comparable to left- or right-handedness. It seemed, further, that there was little hope that many homosexuals could become heterosexual because of the limited therapeutic knowledge available to help them. The life style of the homosexual is at best inconvenient and at worst fraudulent, but this is caused by societal strictures rather than homosexuality itself; thus, concern and pastoral care are due the homosexual. Having so concluded, Stewart felt ready for a talk with Harper.

He called, arranged for an appointment in his study, and the interview began in pleasant fashion. The tone changed quickly, however, as soon as the pastor mentioned the anonymous letters and the concern of the board members.

Harper: (looking angry and stirring in his chair) Those lousy . . .! Wouldn't you know! My friends! . . . my good Christian friends! (calming) It makes me sick inside to think that people can act that way.
Pastor: I know how this must make you feel and I certainly understand your anger. But the board members had genuine concern . . . .
Harper: Did they? Or were they worried about their good names and their reputations and what people would say?
Pastor: Well, I guess there were a lot of reasons they might have had. But at least I want to help you in any way I can. And that's why I wanted to talk to you today. I . . . .
Harper: You're sure you're not here under orders from them? . . . Oh, I don't mean that; I know you want to help. (long pause) What do you want to know—whether it's true—whether or not I am a homosexual? (long pause. Pastor Stewart remains silent.) Well, I am. And now what do we do?

Pastor Stewart was shaken as Harper left his study. It had been a long conference. Despite his preparation for the meeting, he had a hidden hope that Harper would disprove all the rumors. But Harper had been honest. He stated his homosexuality, admitted the trips to Washington, and held to his position without bitterness. There was a sadness as he left, although he agreed to another meeting with the pastor the next day.

Pastor Stewart had to decide on a course of action. He felt himself able to accept Harper and his homosexuality. There were elements in it he couldn't understand as yet and he wanted more time to talk with Harper. But as of this moment he was ready to stand with Harper.

Other problems loomed for Stewart, however, beyond his personal concern for Harper, and this is where future action became important. While the pastor could count on some board and congregational members for support, whatever position he took, he was certain that most of the board members and congregation would expect him to take a firm stand against homosexuality and to remove Harper from the board as quietly and quickly as possible. The pastor is, in members' eyes, the titular head of the congregation and its spiritual leader; therefore, he needs to act "for the good of the congregation." The pastor needed to see how the board members were thinking and what might be known within the congregation. He called a special board meeting for that evening.

As he was shaving, preparatory to the meeting, Pastor Stewart had another thought which troubled him. That afternoon he had spoken to Harper as a pastor counseling a parishioner. During that session, Harper confessed to Stewart that he was a homosexual. But could Pastor Stewart reveal this admission to the church board? Furthermore, at the board meeting, Stewart would be in a different role, that of administrator, and this role had its own obligations. Could one role not know what the other role knew? The only way Pastor Stewart could think to solve this problem was to ask Harper for permission to reveal the fact of his homosexuality to the church board. So Stewart called Harper on the phone and asked for permission. But by now Harper had stiffened his position and the answer to the pastor was, "If the board wants to deal in rumors and anonymous letters, then let them deal with them," but they would have no word from him. Furthermore, he would not attend the board meeting.

The official board session that evening was stormy. Several members, on the basis of the rumors, wanted to remove Harper from the official body. Others expressed strong feelings against his homosexuality but were not certain his removal from the board was the way to handle it. One or two members felt he should have a hearing and then a decision should be made. A few members said nothing. Pastor Stewart led the meeting in a subdued fashion, listened, and gave the general impression that he was reluctant to take either a position or any immediate action. "It is, after all," he said, "mostly at the rumor stage"—and he felt a twinge of guilt as he said it. The meeting seemed to come to one conclusion: the pastor needed to have complete information so that something could be done. How soon would the pastor act? When could this business be finished?

It is obvious that Pastor Stewart, except for the study which he made about homosexuality, was reacting to events rather than creating a climate in which events could be handled. Torn by the several roles he was trying to fulfill, he came under increasing pressure from the expectations of those about him as to what he should do. In the desperate search to find himself, he was impervious to the needs and tensions of others. Until he could find himself, he would be unable to help either his board members or Harper. At the moment, the situation seemed to be one of difficult and unredeemable crisis.

As the night wore on, Stewart was increasingly aware of his own problem and the necessity for a different approach. He concluded that he needed help. Early the next morning he called a friend who had advanced training in counseling and worked part-time in a pastoral counseling center. At 9:00 A.M. he met with the counselor.

Pastor Stewart explained the problem and his own feelings of indecision and frustration about it. The following exchange occurred at one point in the discussion:

Counselor: Now let me just review and highlight what you've said, to see if I have it straight. (The counselor makes a review of the problem.) Is that it?

Stewart: Yes, that's it. And what do I do about it? I have to see Harper this afternoon.

Counselor: OK. Let's take the problem and let me do a little interpreting of it and see if this helps us. The precipitating problem is homosexuality. But as I see it, that's not the root problem for you at the moment. The root problem is the internal confusion you have about the varying roles you feel you're playing, and the expectancies you think the varying members of your board and congregation have for you in dealing with the problem. You are, in other words, somewhat like Riesman's outer-directed man with your radar revolving like mad! It strikes me, then, that until you get this internal problem resolved, you're not going to be able to handle the presenting problem very well.

Stewart: I'm aware of that. And I know you're right. But in another sense, it's the nature of homosexuality that creates the problem for me. I can't think of another issue about which people get so uptight and unreasonable. So if I come out supporting Harper, people will say I'm supporting homosexuality, and if I just let events happen without giving direction, they'll—I'm certain of this—throw him off the church board and then ask me to pick up the pieces.

Counselor: So the center of the problem for you is: If you listen to the vocal members of the congregation, you'll be safe—but to be safe, it would require that you sacrifice Harper. Or isn't that a sacrifice?

Stewart: Wow! When you put it that way, the direction I was going doesn't sound as good as I thought.

Counselor: And if it doesn't sound as good, then what sounds better in your mind?

Stewart: Well, you know . . . it suddenly strikes me that I haven't asked the important question. I've been listening to everyone and trying to please everyone and . . . well, I haven't asked myself what I should have . . . .

Counselor: . . . which is?

Stewart: Well, what is right? . . . What is the Christian thing to do? What the Christian attitude and approach should be to this problem.

Counselor: . . . and what is that?

Stewart: Well, I think the Christian action should be to accept and support Harper and offer him pastoral care, the same as would be offered to any other member with a problem.

Counselor: Even at the expense of alienation . . . and your own personal position?

Stewart: Yes, even at that.

The session terminated shortly after this point in their discussion and Stewart went home to prepare for the afternoon meeting with Harper. He resolved to assume a leadership position by emphasizing his role as pastor and by being a counselor to Harper and others who needed him. He was aware of the expectancies of many in the congregation, but felt that a Christian concern for the persons involved, rather than a Christian stance on the issues, could override the opposing pressures. He would do, as he said, "the Christian thing." So he invited Harper to his office and after some preliminary discussion the following exchange took place:

Harper: Well, in any case, I've calmed down a bit and I'm ready to talk about the problem I seem to have caused.

Stewart: Good. And I want you to know that I am ready to go to bat for you in any way that I can.

Harper: In any way that you can? What do you mean by that? Go to bat in any way that you can?

Stewart: (hesitantly) Well . . . you know . . . there are some who want to have you, uh . . . well . . . leave the board if you are homosexual. And I want you to know that I feel you should remain as a member of the church board even if it becomes known that you are a homosexual.

Harper: Why? Why do you want me to remain?

Stewart: Because . . . well, because you need support at this moment, when people are attacking you; to give in to them unthinkingly is both dishonest and unchristian, and I'm ready to support you.

Harper: I'm really not sure I understand all this. I am to be removed from the church board if I am a homosexual—right? OK—now what have I done that is terrible enough to remove me from the board as . . . as unfit? I know that people . . . well, what have I done?

Stewart: You're pressing me rather hard, John, and I do want you to know I'm with you . . . but, in answering your question . . . it's, I guess, being with the homosexual group in Washington that brings the thing to a head. That, and what some of the people in the church feel about homosexuality. You understand what these feelings are . . . .

Harper: Boy, do I ever understand! So my being with a homosexual group in Washington is what's wrong . . . well, is that unusual for a homosexual? What do some of your heterosexual men do when they go to Washington? . . . or Minneapolis?

Stewart: I know that and I can appreciate your feelings. But in their eyes it's different . . . .

Harper: In their eyes . . . how about your eyes? You're ready to defend me, you say . . . as a Christian. But if I hear you right, you're defending me as a person—me, John Harper—which I appreciate; but you're not dealing with John Harper, the homosexual person; just John Harper. And for me, that's not enough. Now don't get me wrong. I'm not trying to be militant about homosexuality. I'm simply trying to say that I want to be accepted *with* my warts. And can your Christian view stretch all the way from John Harper, the person, to John Harper, the homosexual person?

Stewart: John, I hear you. And I think my answer is yes. But you've got to be a little accepting of me at this point. I'm dealing with you in an area that I know little about in any real sense. I've started with you. Be patient with me as I try to get beyond that.

The Active Stance in Counseling

The pastor matured as a counselor during this session. He offered a type of acceptance to Harper—"ready to go to bat for you"—and Harper rejected it. The offer was thinly conceived. A homosexual lives with scorn, rebuke, and guilt. He learns to view skeptically any easy acceptance, for too often in his experience such acceptance proves to be one more veiled rebuke. So Harper rejected Stewart's approach—"I want to be accepted *with* my warts"—and forced the pastor to recognize the limits of his offer. Harper also brought out the issue behind the discussion: How far can Christianity go toward accepting homosexuality?

Behind the interchange between the pastor and Harper was a subtle breakdown in the counseling relationship which Stewart began to recognize. Fundamental to any counseling relationship is the creation of a facilitative base through empathy, genuineness, and concreteness. In each facilitative element there is a quality of unconditionality; the counselor goes with his counselee wherever that might be. Carl Rogers expresses this in his definition of empathy: "The state of empathy, or being empathic, is to perceive the internal frame of reference of another with accuracy and with the emotional components which pertain thereto, as if one were the other person, but without ever losing the 'as if' condition."[3] Stewart's response to Harper was conditional. The "as if" in the definition was too large, brought on by the pastor's lingering consciousness of his leadership role and the expectancies of the congregation.

Furthermore, Stewart neglected the facilitative expression of concreteness in his counseling. To Harper, Stewart's offer of support was vague and inconclusive. The pastor, in Harper's eyes, did not sense the magnitude of the problem. Harper did not feel that any real solution would be reached simply by talking about "the right and Christian thing to do."

It would be easy for Pastor Stewart at this point to feel hostile and trapped. He could, on the one hand, be angry at Harper for his intransigent position on homosexuality and the refusal to accept offers of help. He could, on the other hand, vent his anger on those board members and members of the congregation who seem determined to drive John off the church board without considering him as a fellow Christian and human being. Most of all, Stewart could resent the variety of roles his ministry requires and the varying demands of members about his performance in those roles.

But Pastor Stewart chooses a different course. He decides to move his counseling and pastoral care into an active mode. First, he needs to delineate, with as much precision as possible, the important issues involved in the situation. Second, he must meet with the church board and establish an appropriate course of

3. Carl Rogers, "A Theory of Therapy, Personality, and Interpersonal Relationships, as Developed in the Client-centered Framework," *Psychology: A Study of a Science,* ed. Sigmund Koch, vol. 3 (New York: McGraw-Hill, 1959), p. 210.

action. Finally, he plans to meet with Harper and deal with the total problem of life style as well as his position on the official church board.

Stewart's decision to give an active thrust to his counseling and pastoral care is indicative of a new and vital development in "the care of souls."[4] The history of pastoral care and counseling is one of quietism and subdued concern. Its concentration has been on the healing of wounds, often a matter of resigned adjustment. At its best such care means a wholesome acceptance of the individual and a reassuring voice in an unfriendly and malevolent world. But in daily operation, quietistic pastoral care can become a form of "pie in the sky" which underscores the future at the expense of the present and results in overaccommodating and overvaluing of the status quo.

Pastoral counseling occurs within a social context and the counselee's problem has social implications which can be both the source of the problem and the roadblock to its solution. At such a point, the pastoral counselor remembers that he stands also in a prophetic tradition. He needs to react not only to the counselee's problem but also to the social malignancy which creates and sustains the problem. It is the recognition of this prophetic-counselor role which moves the pastor from role diffusion to role fusion; now what he does has unified voice and behavioral expresson.

Moving from the quietistic to the active mode in counseling also allows the pastoral counselor to be eclectic and selective in counseling methods. Just as pastoral care tended in the past to be quietly accepting, so pastoral counseling moved to the client-centered nondirective methods. Historically, the adoption of the nondirective method was a necessary corrective to the authoritarian, content-centered approach so widely used by the clergy. For the first time, by using a nondirective approach, the pastoral counselor learned to be quiet and to listen and respond to

4. Wayne E. Oates, *Pastoral Counseling in Social Problems* (Philadelphia: Westminster Press, 1966). See also, Harvey Seifert and Howard J. Clinebell, Jr., *Personal Growth and Social Change* (Philadelphia: Westminster Press, 1969).

his counselee. But granted this advantage, two disadvantages quickly appeared. First, a sense of role diffusion occurred within the pastor himself. Active and directive in the pulpit, as the role of preacher required, he found himself silenced in his role as counselor, blocked by his nondirective method from giving active expression to concerns important to his summary role as pastor. Second, the limitations of the method itself created limitations in its usefulness. The reason for failure is obvious: problems and people are asked to fit a single counseling method rather than letting the counseling method fit the people and their problems.

When, then, the pastoral counselor moves from a quietistic single-method to an active approach in his counseling, he discovers new methods available such as those provided by behavior therapy and rational-emotive psychotherapy (all illustrated in previous chapters). These new methods, holding to relationship principles found in client-centered therapy, allow the pastoral counselor to be eclectic in selecting the best method for the person and the problem presented to him. Thus, in both method and pastoral role, the counseling pastor becomes a "total person" in dealing with his counselee's problems and the society which helps to produce them.[5]

Principles of Affirmation

So Pastor Stewart, in new expression, turns to review the fundamental issues pertinent to the current crisis.

First, the church is fully human and fully in the world. This means that Christian faith and hope—and the Christians who believe and hope—are always on pilgrimage and never at the goal. Somewhat less than the ultimate best is the reality of the church. To suggest that the church is an island of sacredness in the midst of secularity is to renew and reemphasize the dualistic separation of body and spirit which has long afflicted thinking

---

5. For an amplified discussion of the movement toward action and varied methods in pastoral counseling, see Chapter 3, "A Revised Model for Pastoral Counseling" in Howard J. Clinebell, Jr., *Basic Types of Pastoral Counseling* (Nashville: Abingdon Press, 1966).

about the church as well as about human sexuality. The problem of homosexuality comes into the church, then, as one element within the larger picture of human sexuality, a fully human and worldly matter. Individuals within the church will react to homosexuality, not on the basis of a fulfilled Christianity, but on the basis of where they are in their Christian understanding and what they have learned in the culture. The important principle is that the issue be open to discussion and reaction, not glossed over or excluded under the pretense that it does not exist. Homosexuality, as all human sexuality, is a social concern of importance to Christian faith and conscience as surely as bombings, work laws, women's rights, and racial discrimination.

Second, while the church is in the world, it also has something unique to say to the world, and to itself. What is unique is the church's gospel. The gospel, epitomized by love, must be expressed even where it becomes a scandal in the eyes of those who would prefer its exclusion from particular issues. The task of the Christian is to:

> . . . speak of what everyone really knows would be the good. Their contribution is in speaking it, out loud; in speaking it when everyone has agreed to keep silent; in saying "Do it!" when everyone is making thoughts about balancing idealism with practical necessities; in speaking it . . . when everyone is hiding behind abstract definitions of love that excuse from action.[6]

The gospel is the peculiar address made to the issues which come to the church from the world, both inside and outside the church. It is in this address that translation is made of the gospel-meaning for contemporary issues.

Third, human sexuality cannot be restricted to a set pattern. Despite restrictive attempts made throughout the centuries by secular and religious moralists, human sexuality has found ways to express itself. Such expression has often been good, a manifestation of God's creation and gift. But, as with all powerful forces,

---

6. Robert W. Jenson, *Story and Promise* (Philadelphia: Fortress Press, 1973), p. 87.

it has also had its tragic moments in waywardness and variant forms. The negative strain of the biblical-theological tradition emphasizes the waywardness of human sexuality; rooted in Greek dualism and horror of the passionate irrational, it has predominated in both culture and church. The affirmative biblical-theological tradition in human sexuality is rooted in Hebraic custom and comes to fruition in the gospel of love, concern for persons, and freedom from law. Effective translation of this biblical-theological tradition for contemporary man requires words of accountable affirmation rather than restrictive disaffirmation on the part of the counseling pastor.

Fourth, homosexuality is viewed in contemporary culture as a variant and, often, despised form of sexual expression. No matter that its inception, continuance, and expression are bounded by uncertainty in the behavioral sciences; homosexuality and the homosexual meet with disapproval and demands for change. To deal with homosexuality without recognizing this societal derogation is unrealistic. Yet for the Christian, compassion and concern must be involved at the point of judgment. The homosexual is a person. Homosexuality as a sexual expression must stand no less a test than the accountable affirmation asked of, and given to, heterosexuality.

Operational Approaches

With the fundamental issues clarified, Pastor Stewart brought to the board meeting two proposals. The first was to institute as soon as possible a series of small group discussions on the subject, "The Church: Those Who Belong and Those Who Don't." Study would focus on the church as it struggles between one pole of acceptability in the name of Christ and the other pole of noninclusion in the name of society and culture. The first polarity would consider what acceptability means to those who have been "accepted." The second polarity would center on those who are outside the membership of the average congregation, the divergent racial strains, the poor, singles, and homosexuals. The purpose of the discussions would be to broaden the base of acceptance within the church by recognizing how societal attitudes get tangled up with the gospel. Coordinated with this study would be certain emphases in the sermons and discussions in church school classes and in the various church organizations. In proposing this study project, Pastor Stewart was aware of the necessity for open discussion and communication at all levels of church life. Prejudice, ill will, and ignorance could be isolated in such discussions and opportunity opened for efforts to discover and implement appropriate Christian attitudes.

The pastor's second proposal was for the official church board to go on record in support of John Harper without further inquiry into the rumors of homosexuality. The board could, of course, support Harper by taking no action, since John was a board member at the moment. But even if the attacks on Harper were not matters of record, the statement of affirmation would be a public declaration of position.

An affirmative statement of support was important to Pastor Stewart. It would show the church board as an acting body rather than a passive standby group. Most of all, the action would speak against the cruelty of society, and even of the church, when it isolates those who do not meet the current standards of conformity. To ostracize Harper because some, even a majority, feel he does not "fit" is to expose him to the virulent possibility of personality disintegration. To support Harper is to speak the gospel of love even if that speaking is a scandal to those who prefer not to hear it.

The church board reacted as Stewart expected. Several members were visibly angry and thought an investigation should be made of the rumors. But the pastor persisted in his position, emphasizing the principles basic to the issue. After lengthy discussion, the board approved both proposals although three board members registered negative votes on the proposal to support Harper. Pastor Stewart knew the issue was not settled, but at least it was now out in the open, sides were chosen, and continued discussion was feasible.

The next morning the pastor called Harper and an appointment was made for that evening. The central part of their conversation follows.

Pastor: John, as I told you on the phone this morning, the board voted to affirm you as a member last evening. I think it was a very significant move on the board's part.

Harper: It was. And I'm pleased and, I must admit, surprised. I thought they would be after my neck . . . yet it's hard to say that because I always felt those men were my friends. But I can't help but wonder how they would have voted if they had known for sure that I was homosexual. I've wondered since we talked if I, or you, should have told them.

Pastor: That's difficult to say. Sometimes you can say more than people are ready to hear and it doesn't help. But it is a matter to think about for the future.

Harper: Speaking of the future, what about it? Where are we, really? What about my trips to Washington? Should I stop . . . if I can?

Pastor: I've done a lot of thinking about this and I'm going to make a speech. I know that isn't good counseling at first glance. But let's say that it's educative counseling—that clears my professional conscience.

Harper: OK. Speak on!

Pastor: Well . . . John, I know what society does to homosexuals and how that must make you feel . . . and certainly, what problems that creates for you. But I know you well enough to be aware of what kind of a person you are and . . . well, how all this fuss must press on you. But what I want to do is to talk to you as a person, homosexual, heterosexual, sexual, whatever. It strikes me that at some points it's all the same, despite what differences society puts on it.

There are two things most important, I believe: one is your growth as a person—as a Christian, in fact; and the other is the meaning of relationship. And both of these are tied together.

Your growth as a person and as a Christian, first: In the area of sexuality—and that's where we are—I think of your trips to Washington. Is anyone being hurt here, including yourself, by those trips in an exploitive sense. Are you using someone—or allowing yourself to be used?

Harper: You mean sexual contacts—using people for that?

Pastor: Yes—just as I would say this to a heterosexual going anywhere with the same intent. Now I don't expect you to answer me—I'm throwing out questions and ideas to you. But what I am suggesting is:

given the social restrictions, what is responsible homosexuality as sexual expression? How does it lend itself to you for your development as a person?

Harper: That's a new way to put it. I never thought I would hear a pastor say that!

Pastor: I'm not sure I would have ever thought it or said it before this incident! But I wrote down a phrase the other night and I'm trying to apply it to your situation. It's the phrase, "accountable affirmation." Accountable in the sense that you must answer to yourself, to others in contact with you, and to your Christian faith. Exploitive or not? That's first.

Second, personality growth is always a matter of other people. It's an outgrowth of genuine relationship with others. I'm sure you've had that here in this church. But there's also the sexual aspect of relationship. Somehow, I think, the heterosexual pattern has much to say to the homosexual pattern. By that I mean, relationship of a responsible nature is as important to you as it is to me. And that's the end of the speech.

Harper: (long pause) Well, you're right. That was a speech. And it hit home. But I have thought many times about the things you've just said. And I am concerned about myself—and others—and being a Christian—and being a homosexual. You see, I know those people and they're a cross section of the world just as this church is. Good —bad—sick—and not sick. And what you're saying is what I have wished for—and still want. And it's good to hear you say it. And if I haven't said it before, I'll say it now: Thanks so much for what you've done. And thank the board members.

Three days following the discussion, Pastor Stewart received a call from Harper saying that he was going on a week's vacation to think things over. Harper also said that he was thinking about the possibility of resigning from the church board as a way of easing the problem for everyone. Pastor Stewart urged Harper to discuss that move with him before taking it. But, as in the last counseling session with Harper, the pastor hung up the phone still unable in his own mind to affirm homosexuality as such. He would need to think about it much more. Culture and negative traditions wear deep ruts in the soul.

7. Epilogue: Translating the Christian Tradition Today

The counseling pastor's role as translator of the Christian tradition is vitally important to the life and ministry of the church today. Obviously, any pastor who neglects this role diminishes the peculiar demand of his calling. What may be less evident to him and to others is the value of this translation for a culture caught up in a sexual revolution.

This sexual revolution—or better, the explicit sexual emphasis today—has created a new form of devotion which places an almost pristine and consecrated emphasis upon sexuality itself, apart from the rest of life. The doing of the act and its accompanying sensations become a form of monastic service in the name of open sexuality with its promise of ultimate meaning for human life. Thus, in colonies for singles, the search for meaning settles into a game of "scoring" in which the goal is not just the playing of the game but amassing a winning total based on the number of beddings-down achieved. Swingers join this numbers-oriented cult, informing social investigators that the quantity of sexual expression improves the quality of their existential aloneness in the marriage bed. Hard-core pornography adds its sensualities to this emphasis by exaggerating responses, sizes, desires, and situations until fantasy seduces reality, and the participant seeks sensations that always elude the grasp.

The pastor has always been a translator of the Christian tradition to a world that searches for meaning. But when that world has searched for the meaning of sexuality, the traditional Christian response has been too often a negative voice for repression. Such a negative voice fails to answer the question of meaning; in addition, it proves to be of limited usefulness in dealing with expressions of sexuality. Repression always runs the danger of

113

creating a Victorian-like society which builds a structure of stylized gentility over a substructure of vice and human bestiality. Repression of the act never stops the thought which gives birth to it. Yet the alternative—license—in an area of such great importance to persons and their lives is equally unpalatable, and still fails to answer the question of meaning.

The pastoral counselor's task of translation is essential because, through recognizing the vigorous affirmation of sexuality within the Christian tradition, he provides an answer to the sexual searchings of today. This translation of affirmation acknowledges the importance of sexuality without resorting to the extremes of libertinism or repressive closure.

The diverse aspects of Christian affirmation become important, then, to the interpretation which the pastoral counselor brings to each problem of sexuality. While the translation may have varied points at which to begin, the most suggestive point is with the person himself. This is useful, not only in itself, but also in reminding the pastor that the purpose of the translation is to help the individual with his problem and not just as a translation exercise alone.

The Christian affirmation of sexuality begins with the view of man as a whole being. This was the thrust in the Hebraic view of sexuality and much of the early Christian tradition, particularly in the Gospels. The insistence on the wholeness of the person in sexuality is a fundamental response to contemporary sexual revolutionists who attempt to separate sexuality and the activities of sex from all other aspects of the person. A Christian affirmation insists that sexuality dare not be reduced to the hasty coupling of genital organs, for a whole man and a whole woman are involved in the act. To ignore this wholeness, even though a relationship be stamped and certified by bell, book, and candle, is to create a demeaning exploitation and a diminution of the person.

The wholeness of the person is a fundamental perspective for newer understandings of sex role socialization. Roles forced by culture on men and women—the ever aggressive male and the meek, submissive female—are expressions of fragmentation in human life. The inevitable result of such role structure in sexuality is to demean the male by allowing him no emotional outlet except strident lust ("I have needs to be met") and to circumscribe the female by discouraging personal expression except as sex object for that masculine need ("He goes wild when I wear this perfume"). That a man might be lovingly tender and a woman lovingly assertive appears too often in contemporary classification to be both paradoxical and abnormal.

The Christian affirmation of wholeness reproves the sexual revolutionist who seeks to isolate the part from the whole. Yet such an affirmation also speaks decisively to the sexual traditionalist who uses the part to categorize the whole. The Gospel incident of the woman taken in adultery is markedly different in its concept of wholeness from Hawthorne's *The Scarlet Letter,* where Hester Prynne was personified totally by the letter *A* worn on her dress. In the biblical account, Jesus viewed the woman as a whole person *not unlike* those who stood ready to stone her. While he judged her part in adultery as sin, he refused to allow that one act to overshadow her personhood. In contrast, the puritan community looked upon Hester and perceived only her act of adultery, ignoring her as a person. The pastoral counselor sees evidence of the part categorizing the whole when he hears one spouse declare a marriage ended because of an act of infidelity on the part of the other spouse. The total marriage is judged by one behavioral incident.

This tendency to use the part to circumscribe the whole in sexuality creates many of the problems for singles in society. Sexual intimacy, even responsibly undertaken, is labeled as sinful and immoral without regard to the limitations on wholeness of personality forced on the single person by society.

The second major aspect in Christian affirmation about sexuality is in the realm of relationships. When Jesus summarized the Mosaic law, he spoke in terms of right relationship to God and to neighbor. If sexuality is the good gift of God in creation, as the Hebrew people saw it, then this good gift finds expression within caring human relationships. Hence the quality of relationship becomes the vital ingredient in human sexuality.

The pastoral counselor, in expressing the affirmation of right relationship, speaks to this issue without condemning automatically any contact between persons which carries a sexual overtone. Where there is concern, love, and commitment in a relationship, sexual or not, there is the right relationship which Jesus recognized and approved.

Failure in relationship may reveal to the pastoral counselor the tragic elements of sexual deviation. In situations such as fetishism or voyeurism, there can be no rightful relationship because unhappy needs drive the person toward a fulfillment of self with little regard for other persons. Again the affirmation of wholeness reminds the pastor that, when proper referral is made to professional therapists for help, the person with the deviation continues to be the object of Christian love and concern.

Finally, the Christian affirmation of wholeness and relationship extends to the counseling pastor himself. It is not surprising to discover the high correlation between the Christian affirmations in sexuality and the necessary attributes for the good counselor: acceptance, understanding, and genuineness. But such attributes of good counseling in the field of human sexuality are difficult to attain if the counselor holds to a negative view of sexuality or if he has problems with his own sexuality. No matter how hard the pastor may try, his negative views or his own problems will intervene to block his expression of genuineness, acceptance, or understanding of the counselee. And even where the pastor does deal with sexuality in an affirmative fashion and does strive to be a genuine person in his counseling relationships, he faces the possibility of clash with varying congregational expectations and viewpoints.

It should not be surprising, then, that counseling in matters of sexuality will raise difficult problems for the pastor. The move away from negativism and legalism does not occur easily or without surges of anxiety and fear, for no society can endure without knowing the limitations to its sexual conduct. The counseling pastor who holds to affirmations of sexuality from the Christian tradition not only communicates crucial values for the lives of the people to whom he ministers, but also speaks to the future of both church and society in matters of sexuality. His task of translation is ongoing as he affirms principles and guidelines derived from the gospel—of good news—and works creatively to bring about life-enriching sexual attitudes and behavior.

Yet as the counseling pastor translates the tradition to society, he also bears responsibility for keeping the tradition informed by the behavioral sciences and relevant to a changing society. Only through reciprocal flow of guidance and information will both church and society receive the important contributions each has to offer to the understanding of human sexuality. The pastor, in dealing with human sexuality, moves in a frontier area of counseling where tradition and culture struggle toward the abundant life. In this frontier, he is the central figure.

Bibliography for Further Study

Christianity and Sex

Blenkinsopp, Joseph. *Sexuality and the Christian Tradition*. Dayton, Ohio: Pflaum Press, 1969.
This book is valuable for its insightful theological approach to the erotic aspect of human sexuality.

Cole, William G. *Sex in Christianity and Psychoanalysis*. New York: Oxford University Press, 1955.
An intensive study of historical Christian interpretations of sex, beginning with Jesus and continuing through the Reformation to survey contemporary Protestant and Catholic viewpoints. On the basis of historical Christian background and the psychoanalytic interpretations of human sexuality, Cole attempts a critical reconstruction of a Christian view of sex.

Denominational Church Statements

Francoeur, Robert T. *Eve's New Rib*. New York: Harcourt Brace Jovanovich, 1972.
Francoeur, who is trained in biology and theology, has written a provocative book in which he explores a new approach to education in human sexuality and thoughtfully examines the impact of technology and future shock on our traditional sexual mores.

Hiltner, Seward. *Sex Ethics and the Kinsey Reports*. New York: Association Press, 1953.
A clear and careful analysis of the Kinsey studies written with a view toward suggesting a contemporary Christian view of sexuality. The discussion goes well beyond the confines of Kinsey.

Mace, David R. *The Christian Response to the Sexual Revolution*. Nashville: Abingdon Press, 1970.
A short, very readable book which points out the antisexual bias in the Christian tradition and calls for a positive Christian response to the sexual revolution which grounds itself in the Doctrine of Creation and the Doctrine of the Incarnation.

Roy, Rustum and Della. *Honest Sex*. New York: New American Library, 1972.
This book is radical in the best sense of that word. In groping for a Christian perspective toward contemporary sexuality, the Roys ex-

plore creatively the implications of relationships built on Christian
agape. Their viewpoint toward the single person is both sympathetic
and provocative.

Thielicke, Helmut. *The Ethics of Sex.* Trans. John W. Doberstein. New
York: Harper and Row, 1964.
An extensive treatment of sexual ethics derived from anthropology,
psychology, and biblical interpretation. His sections on homosexuality
and birth control are good.

Wood, Frederic C., Jr. *Sex and the New Morality.* New York: Association Press, 1968.
Moving from the premise that sexuality is both mysterious and complex, Wood, a college chaplain, speaks for a person-centered,
Christian/humanist ethic in relation to sexual attitudes and behavior.

Human Sexuality

Karlen, Arno. *Sexuality and Homosexuality: A New View.* New York:
W. W. Norton and Co., 1971.
A profuse and comprehensive review of attitudes and viewpoints
about homosexuality, transvestism, transexualism, and other variant
forms of sexual behavior. Karlen includes historical, transcultural, and
multidisciplinary perspectives.

Mace, David R. *Sexual Difficulties in Marriage.* Philadelphia: Fortress
Press, 1972.
A very helpful book from the Pocket Counsel Series, which can be
utilized by the pastor in assigning supplementary reading for the
couple experiencing sexual difficulties.

Masters, William H., and Johnson, Virginia E. *Human Sexual
Inadequacy.* Boston: Little, Brown and Co., 1970.
This technical work is basic for an understanding of the processes and
problems in the physiological expression of sexuality. It proposes
counseling approaches to problems which the pastor may want to
utilize.

Wrage, Karl, M.D. *Man and Woman.* Philadelphia: Fortress Press,
1969.
A well-illustrated guide to the basics of sex and marriage. It is written
with sensitivity to the emotional and spiritual needs of men and women
as it deals with the physiology of sex and the development of sexuality
through childhood, adolescence, and childbirth.

Sexuality and Sex Roles

Bernard, Jessie S. *The Future of Marriage.* New York: World Publishing Co., 1972.

A prophetic look at the future of male-female relationships in the light of our changing society.

Daly, Mary. *The Church and the Second Sex*. New York: Harper and Row, 1968.

A critical examination of Christian thought and history as it has traditionally assigned women a secondary place in the life of the church.

Doely, Sarah Bentley, ed. *Women's Liberation and the Church*. New York: Association Press, 1970.

A collection of essays representing various concerns and experiences of women as they struggle to be truly free in the Christian church today.

Friedan, Betty. *The Feminine Mystique*. New York: Dell Publishing Co., 1964.

One of the first books to look seriously at the American woman in terms of sex role socialization and its glaring inadequacies. An excellent resource for understanding the "housewife's syndrome."

Janeway, Elizabeth. *Man's World, Woman's Place: A Study in Social Mythology*. New York: William Morrow and Co., 1971.

Here the author examines the social mythology underlying traditional male-female roles and relationships. Her analysis is perceptive and is carried out with major emphasis on the emotional drives which sustain the social myths, even in the face of radical role change for contemporary women.

General Counseling Approaches

Clinebell, Howard J., Jr. *Basic Types of Pastoral Counseling*. Nashville: Abingdon Press, 1966.

A fundamental resource for the pastor which offers both a model for pastoral counseling and basic descriptions of varying counseling methodologies.

Hauck, Paul A. *Reason in Pastoral Counseling*. Philadelphia: Westminster Press, 1972.

The first book to deal with rational-emotive psychotherapy and its use by the pastoral counselor. It is clearly written with many illustrative cases.

Lazarus, Arnold A. *Behavior Therapy and Beyond*. New York: McGraw-Hill, 1971.

Basic to understanding the concepts and practice of behavior therapy, the book also shows the newer areas into which behavior therapy is moving. While explicit and detailed, it is easily read by one unacquainted with the subject.

Seifert, Harvey, and Clinebell, Howard J., Jr. *Personal Growth and Social Change.* Philadelphia: Westminster Press, 1969.
An enlightening exploration of the role of the minister as a change agent. The book is particularly helpful in showing clergymen how to make the move from a passive to an active stance in pastoral care and counseling.

Wolpe, J., and Lazarus, A. A. *Behavior Therapy Techniques.* New York: Pergamon, 1966.
The book does what the title says: it explains and illustrates a number of techniques in behavior therapy. Case studies help the reader to get the "feel" of this approach.